Grant Allen

The Colours of Flowers

As illustrated in the British Flora

Grant Allen

The Colours of Flowers
As illustrated in the British Flora

ISBN/EAN: 9783337107499

Printed in Europe, USA, Canada, Australia, Japan

Cover: Foto ©ninafisch / pixelio.de

More available books at **www.hansebooks.com**

NATURE SERIES.

THE
COLOURS OF FLOWERS

AS

ILLUSTRATED IN THE BRITISH FLORA

BY

GRANT ALLEN

WITH ILLUSTRATIONS

London
MACMILLAN AND CO.
1882

The Right of Translation and Reproduction is Reserved.

PREFACE.

THE first germ of the theory contained in this little volume was originally set forth as an article in the *Cornhill Magazine*, and I have to thank the courtesy of the Editor and Publishers of that periodical for their kind permission to expand it into its present far fuller form.

I have been encouraged thus to give it shape in a more permanent dress by the friendly appreciation of the late Mr. Darwin, who wrote to me as follows with regard to the central idea of my original paper—the derivation of petals from flattened and abortive stamens:—"Many years ago I thought it highly probable that petals were in all cases transformed stamens. I forget (excepting the water-lily) what made me think so; but I am sure that your evolutionary argument never occurred to me, as it is too striking and too apparently valid ever to be forgotten." It appeared to me that if the idea so commended itself to Mr. Darwin, it might also commend itself to other evolutionary biologists; and I have ventured accordingly to work it out here to its furthest legitimate conclusions.

My acknowledgments are due in the highest degree to Sir John Lubbock's admirable little work on *British Wild Flowers in Relation to Insects*, and to Mr. Bentham's *British Flora*. I also owe much to Sir Joseph Hooker's *Student's Flora*, to Professor Sachs's *Botany*, and to other books too numerous to mention. Personally, I have to thank my friend Mr. F. T. Richards, Tutor of Trinity College, Oxford, for many valuable suggestions and corrections of which I have gladly availed myself.

G. A.

CONTENTS.

CHAPTER I.
THE ORIGIN OF PETALS . . . . PAGE 1

CHAPTER II.
GENERAL LAW OF PROGRESSIVE COLOURATION 17

CHAPTER III.
VARIEGATION 61

CHAPTER IV.
RELAPSE AND RETROGRESSION 71

CHAPTER V.
DEGENERATION 91

CHAPTER VI.
MISCELLANEOUS 110

THE COLOURS OF FLOWERS.

CHAPTER I.

THE ORIGIN OF PETALS.

EVERYBODY knows that flowers are rendered beautiful to us by their shapes, by their perfumes, and above all by their brilliant and varied colours. All people who have paid any attention to botany further know that not every flower is thus bright and conspicuous; as a general rule, only those blossoms which depend for their fertilisation upon the visits of insects are provided with special attractions of honey, scent, and vivid hues. An immense number of flowering plants, perhaps even the majority among them, produce only small and unnoticeable inflorescences, like those of grasses, oaks, conifers, and many other field weeds or forest trees. The flowers that most people observe and recognise as such, are the few highly developed forms which possess large expanded coloured surfaces to allure the eyes of their insect fertilisers. It is with flowers in this more popular and ordinary sense that we shall have to deal mainly in the present little treatise; and our object must be to determine, not why they are all as a group brightly coloured, but why this, that, or the other particular blossom should possess this, that, or the other particular hue. Why is the buttercup yellow, while the stitchwort is white, the dog-rose pink, and the harebell blue? Why is the purple foxglove dappled inside with lurid red spots? Why are the central florets of the daisy yellow, while the ray-florets are pinky-white? Why does sky-blue prevail amongst all the veronicas, while yellow predominates in the St. John's worts, and white in the umbellates? These are the sort of questions which we must endeavour briefly to answer, by the light of modern evolutionary biology, from the point of view of the function which each colour specially subserves in the economy of the particular plant which displays it.

The brilliant pigments of flowers usually reside in the specialised organs known as petals, though they are sometimes also found in the sepals and bracts, or more rarely in the stamens and even in the pistil. For the sake of those readers who happen to be imperfectly acquainted with the subject at large (and also to bring the botanical reader definitely into the required point of view), it may be well to begin with a very brief description of the organs which go to make up a typical flower, together with a short account of the part played by colour in general in the fertilising function.

The essential elements in the flower are not at all the showy and brilliant leaves which we usually associate most with the name, but a set of comparatively small and unnoticeable organs occupying the centre of most ordinary blossoms. The simplest type of flower consists of two such organs only, a pistil or ovary containing an embryo seed, and a stamen which produces the pollen necessary to impregnate it. The production of seed is in fact the sole function of the flower; every additional part is only useful in so far as it conduces to this practical end. In the most simple (though not the most primitive) blossoms, fertilisation is effected by a grain of pollen from a stamen falling upon the stigma or sensitive surface of the pistil, and thence sending forth a pollen-tube, which penetrates the ovule or embryo seed, and so impregnates it.

As a rule, however, it is not desirable that a flower should be fertilised by pollen from its own stamens. Mr. Darwin has shown in many cases that when a pistil is fecundated by pollen from a neighbouring blossom, or still better from a different plant, it sets more and sounder seeds, or produces heartier and stronger young seedlings. To attain the benefits of such cross-fertilisation, many plants have acquired special peculiarities of structure: or, to put it more correctly, those plants which have spontaneously varied in certain favourable directions have been oftenest cross-fertilised, and have thus on the average produced more and stouter offspring. The advantage thus gained in the struggle for existence has enabled them to live down their less adapted compeers, and to hand on their own useful peculiarities to a large number of descendants. There are two ways in which plants have ensured such a benefit; the one is by adapting themselves to fertilisation by means of the wind, the other is by adapting themselves to fertilisation by means of insects. The first class are said to possess anemophilous, the second class entomophilous, flowers.[1] It is with the latter alone that we have here mainly to deal.

Entomophilous or insect-fertilised flowers are those in which the pollen is habitually carried from the stamens of one blossom to the pistil of the next on the head or legs of butterflies, bees, beetles, or other flying arthropods. In order to allure these insects, and to induce them to visit one flower after another of the same kind, the plants have often developed small quantities of honey in the neighbourhood of the essential organs, as well as specially coloured floral leaves known as petals. Accordingly, a fully evolved entomophilous blossom usually consists of the four following whorls, or sets of parts, beginning from within outward. *First*, in the very centre, the pistil, or carpellary whorl, consisting of one or more carpels or ovaries, each containing one or more embryo seeds. *Secondly*, outside the pistil, the staminal whorl, consisting of one or more pollen-bearing stamens, usually three or six in the great class of Monocotyledons, and five or ten in the great class of Dicotyledons. *Thirdly*, outside the stamens, the corolla or petaline whorl, consisting of several separate or united petals, usually three in the Monocotyledons and five in the Dicotyledons. *Fourthly*, outside the corolla, the calyx or sepaline whorl, consisting of several separate or united sepals, usually the same in number as the petals. The position and arrangement

---

[1] For further particulars see Sir John Lubbock's work on *British Wild Flowers in Relation to Insects*, in the Nature Series.

of these parts is shown in the accompanying diagrams (Figs. 1 and 2).

As regards function, the pistil produces the seeds and grows later into the fruit. The stamens produce pollen, to impregnate the pistil. The petals attract the fertilising insects by their bright colour, and advertise the honey, if any. The calyx covers up the flower in the bud, and often serves to protect it

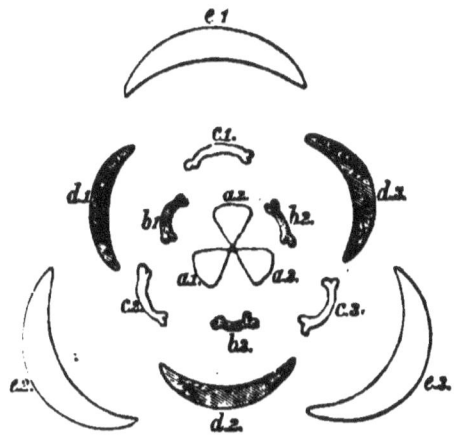

FIG. 1.—Diagram of typical primitive monocotyledonous flower. *a*, carpels; *b*, inner whorl of stamens; *c*, outer whorl of stamens; *d*, petals; *e*, sepals. Each whorl consists of three members.

from the attacks of useless creeping or honey-eating insects.

One more preliminary explanation is necessary before we enter upon the consideration of our main subject. Flowering plants, at a very early date in their history, split up into two great divisions. One of these, the GYMNOSPERMS, to which all the oldest fossil plants belong, as well as our own modern conifers and cycads, possessed and still possess flowers and fruits of a very simple character. Each blossom consists as a rule of a single stamen or a single naked ovule, growing on a scale or an altered leaf; and they display some remarkable analogies with ferns, club-mosses, and other flowerless plants. Of course, they never have petals or coloured organs. The existing Gymnosperms may be regarded as living survivors of a great class, once dominant, but now nearly extinct; and their flowers probably still preserve for us the original type of all blossoms, very

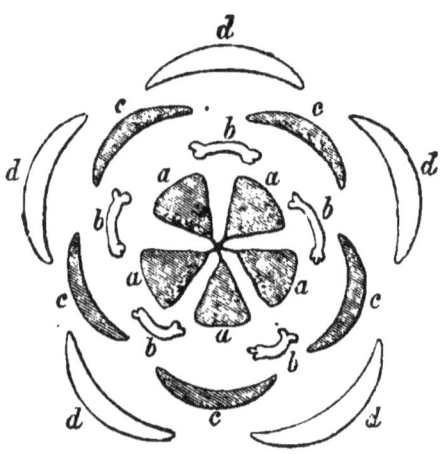

FIG. 2.—Diagram of typical primitive dicotyledonous flower. *a*, carpels; *b*, stamens; *c*, petals; *d*, sepals. Each whorl consists of five members.

slightly altered by time and circumstances. This is especially the case with the cycads, small tropical trees of palm-like appearance, whose inflorescence is the very simplest of all known flowering plants. The other great division, that of the ANGIOSPERMS, has always more fully developed blossoms, often entomophilous, and possessed of brilliant colours. It split up again at an early period of its development into two secondary large classes, those of the *Monocotyledons* and the *Dicotyledons*. These important classes are distinguished from one another by several special points of structure; but the most striking one, so far as regards our present subject, consists in the fact that the Monocotyledons are generally arranged in whorls of threes, while the Dicotyledons are generally arranged in whorls of fives. At the present day, the two modes of arrangement are often obscured in various ways; for example, among some Monocotyledons the stamens are doubled, or consist of two separate whorls, while the petals and sepals are coloured alike and are otherwise almost indistinguishable, so that the flowers seem at first sight to be arranged by sixes rather than by threes; and again, among some Dicotyledons, one or more petals are suppressed, or added, or all the petals are united into a single circular or tubular corolla, so that the arrangement seems at first sight to be by fours, or by eights, or by threes rather than by fives. Originally, however, all Monocotyledons had a trinary arrangement, while all Dicotyledons had a quinary arrangement; and these fundamental plans can still distinctly be traced in by far the larger number of existing species.

So much by way of introduction. Now, since the bright pigments of flowers usually reside in the petals, and since petals have for their main if not for their only function the display of such pigments as an attraction for the fertilising insects, it is clear that we must begin our inquiry by asking,—What was the original colour of the organs from which petals were developed? For we may take it for granted that the primordial petals would at first follow the hue of the part out of which they were originally evolved. For example, if we ought to regard them as altered and modified leaves, then we may fairly conclude that the earliest petals were green; while, if we ought to regard them as altered and modified stamens, then we may fairly conclude that they were yellow. Which of these two alternatives is the most likely to be true? Apparently, the latter.

Petals are in all probability originally enlarged and flattened stamens, which have been set apart for the special work of attracting insects. It seems likely that all flowers at first consisted of the central organs alone—that is to say, of a pistil, which contains the ovary with its embryo seeds; and of a few stamens, which produce the pollen, whose co-operation is necessary in order to fertilise these same embryo ovules and to make the pistil mature into the ripe fruit. But in those plants which took to fertilisation by means of insects—or, one ought rather to say, in those plants which insects took to visiting for the sake of their honey or pollen, and so unconsciously fertilising—the flowers soon began to produce an outer row of barren and specialised stamens, adapted by their size and colour for attracting the fertilising insects; and these barren and specialised stamens are what we commonly call petals. Any flowers which thus presented brilliant masses of colour to allure the eyes of the beetles, the bees, and the butterflies, would naturally receive the greatest number of visits from their insect friends, and would therefore stand the best chance of setting their seeds, as well as of producing healthy and vigorous offspring as the result of a proper cross. In this way, as we have seen, they would gain an advantage in the struggle for life over their less fortunate compeers, and would hand down their own peculiarities to their descendants after them.

But as the stamens of almost all flowers, certainly of all the oldest and simplest flowers, are yellow, it would seem naturally to follow that the earliest petals would be yellow too. When the stamens of the outer row were flattened and broadened into petals, there would be no particular reason why they should change their colour; and, in the absence of any good reason, they doubtless retained it as before. Indeed, we shall see, a little later on, that the earliest and simplest types of existing flowers are almost always yellow, seldom white, and never blue; and this in itself would be a sufficient ground for believing that yellow was the original colour of all petals. But as it is somewhat heretical to believe, contrary to the general run of existing scientific opinion, that petals are derived from flattened stamens, instead of from simplified and attenuated leaves, it may be well to detail here the reasons for this belief, because it seems of capital importance in connection with our present subject; for if the petals were originally a row of altered stamens set apart for the special function of attracting insects, it would be natural and obvious why they should begin by being yellow; but if they were originally a set of leaves, which became thinner and more brightly coloured for the same purpose, it would be difficult to see why they should first have assumed any one colour rather than another.

The accepted doctrine as to the nature of petals is

that discovered by Wolf and subsequently rediscovered by Goethe, after whose name it is usually called; for of course, as in all such cases, the greater man's fame has swallowed up the fame of the lesser. Goethe held that all the parts of the flower were really modified leaves, and that a gradual transition could be traced between them, from the ordinary leaf, through the stem-leaf and the bract, to the sepal, the petal, the stamen, and the ovary or carpel. Now, if we look at most modern flowers, such a transition can undoubtedly be observed; and sometimes it is very delicately graduated, so that you can hardly say where each sort of leaf merges into the next. But, unfortunately for the truth of the theory as ordinarily understood, we now know that in the earliest flowers there were no petals or sepals, but that primitive flowering plants had simply leaves on the one hand, and stamens and ovules on the other. The oldest types of flowers at present surviving are certain Gymnosperms, such as the cycads, of which the well-known *Zamias* of our conservatories may be regarded as good examples. These have only naked ovules on the one hand and clusters of stamens in a sort of cone on the other. The Gymnosperms are geologically earlier than any other flowering plants. But, if petals and sepals are later in origin (as we know them to be) than stamens and carpels, we can hardly say that they mark the transition from one form to the other, any more than we can say that Gothic architecture marks the transition from the Egyptian style to the classical Greek. It is not denied, indeed, that the stamen and the ovary are themselves by origin modified leaves—that part of the Wolfian theory is absolutely irrefutable—but with the light shed upon the subject by the modern doctrine of evolution, we can no longer regard petals and sepals as intermediate stages between the two. The earliest flowering plants had true leaves on the one hand, and specialised pollen-bearing or ovule-bearing leaves on the other hand, which latter are what in their developed forms we call stamens and carpels; but they certainly had no petals at all, and the petals of modern flowers have been produced at some later period. It is probable, too, that they have been produced by a modification of certain external stamens, not by a modification of true leaves. Instead of being leaves arrested on their way towards becoming stamens, they are really stamens which have partially reverted towards the condition of leaves. They differ from true leaves, however, in their thin, spongy texture, and usually in the bright pigments with which they are adorned.

All stamens show a great tendency easily to become petaloid, as it is technically called; that is to say, to flatten out their filament or stalk, and finally to lose their pollen-bearing sacs or anthers. In the waterlilies—which are in certain ways one of the oldest and simplest types of flowers we now possess still preserving many antique points of structure unchanged—we can trace a regular gradation from the perfect stamen to the perfect petal. Take for example our common English white waterlily, *Nymphæa alba* (Fig. 3). In the centre of the flower we find stamens of the ordinary sort, with rounded stalks or filaments, and long yellow anthers full of pollen at the end of each; then, as we move outward, we find the filaments growing flatter and broader, and the pollen-sacs less and less perfect; next we find a few stamens which look exactly like petals, only that they have two abortive anthers stuck awkwardly on to their summits; and, finally, we find true petals, broad and flat, and without any trace of the anthers at all. Here in this very ancient though largely modified flower we have stereotyped for us, as it were, the mode in which stamens first developed into petals, under stress of insect selection.[1]

Fig. 3.—Transition from stamens into petals in white waterlily (*Nymphæa alba*).

"But how do we know," it may be asked, "that the transition was not in the opposite direction? How do we know that the waterlily had not petals alone to start with, and that these did not afterwards develop, as the Wolfian hypothesis would have us believe, into stamens?" For a very simple reason. The theory of Wolf and Goethe is quite incompatible with the doctrine of development, at least if accepted as a

[1] The waterlilies belong to a very ancient type, in some respects partially intermediate between Monocotyledons and Dicotyledons; but the comparative unification of their pistil shows them to have undergone considerable modification.

historical explanation (which Wolf and Goethe of course never meant it to be). Flowers can and do exist without petals, which are no essential part of the organism, but a mere set of attractive coloured advertisements for alluring insects; but no flower can possibly exist without stamens, which are one of the two essential reproductive organs in the plant. Without pollen, no flower can set its seeds. A parallel from the animal world will make this immediately obvious. Hive-bees consist of three kinds—the queens or fertile females, the drones or males, and the workers or neuters. Now it would be absurd to ask whether the queens were developed from an original class of neuters, or the neuters from an original class of fertile females. Neuters left to themselves would die out in a single generation: they are really sterilised females, set apart for a special function on behalf of the hive. It is just the same with petals: they are sterilised stamens, set apart for the special function of attracting insects on behalf of the entire flower. But to ask which came first, the petals or the stamens, is as absurd as to ask which came first, the male and female bees or the neuters.

Indeed, if we examine closely the waterlily petals, it is really quite impossible to conceive of the transition as taking place from petals to stamens instead of from stamens to petals. It is quite easy to understand how the filament of an active stamen may become gradually flattened, and the anthers (or pollen-sacs) progressively void and functionless: but it is very difficult to understand how or why a petal should first begin to develop an abortive anther, and then a partially effective anther, and at last a perfect stamen.

The one change is comprehensible and reasonable, the other change is meaningless and absurd. Of course, it is not intended to deny the truth of Wolf's great generalisation in the way in which he meant it —the existence of a homology between the leaf and all the floral organs: but the conception certainly requires to be modified a little by the light of later evolutionary discoveries. The starting-point consists of a plant having three kinds of organs, true foliage leaves, staminal leaves, and carpellary leaves: the petals and sepals are apparently later intermediate modifications, produced in special connection with the acquired habit of insect fertilisation.

In many other cases besides the waterlily, we know that stamens often turn into petals. Thus the numerous coloured rays of the *Mesembryanthemums* or ice-plant family are acknowledged by many botanists to be flattened stamens. In *Canna*, where one anther-cell is abortive, the filament of the solitary stamen becomes petaloid. In the Ginger order, one outer whorl of stamens resembles the tubular corolla, so that the perianth seems to consist of nine lobes instead of six. In orchids, according to Mr. Darwin, the lip consists of one petal and two petaloid stamens of the outer whorl. In double roses (Fig. 4) and almost all other double flowers the extra petals are produced from the stamens of the interior. In short, stamens generally can be readily converted into petals, especially in rich and fertile soils or under cultivation. The change is extremely common in the families of *Ranunculaceæ, Papaveraceæ, Magnoliaceæ, Malvaceæ*, and *Rosaceæ*, all very simple types. Even where stamens always retain their pollen-sacs, they have often broad, flattened petaloid filaments, as in the star of Bethlehem and many other flowers. The curious scales on the petals of *Parnassia palustris* are now known to be altered stamens. Looking at the question as a whole, we can see how petals might easily have taken their origin from stamens, while it is difficult to understand how they could have taken their origin from ordinary leaves—a process of which, if it ever took place, no hint now remains to us. We shall see hereafter that the manner in which certain outer florets in the compound flower-heads of the daisy or the aster have been sterilised and specialised for the work of

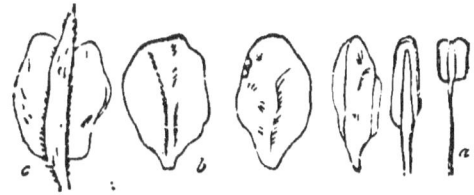

FIG. 4.—Transition from stamen (*a*) to petal (*b*) and sepal (*c*) in flower of double rose.

attraction, affords an exact analogy to the manner in which it is here suggested that certain stamens may at an earlier date have been sterilised and specialised for the same purpose, thus giving rise to what we know as petals.

In a few rare instances, petals even now show a slight tendency to revert to the condition of fertile stamens. In *Monandra fistulosa* the lower lip is sometimes prolonged into a filament bearing an anther: and the petals of shepherd's-purse (*Capsella bursa-pastoris*) have been observed antheriferous.

The hypothesis upon which we shall hereafter

proceed, therefore, will be that petals are really derived from altered stamens. We shall return at a later point to the proofs of this position, and examine a few arguments which may be brought against it. For the present, it will be better to put forward the remainder of our general theory at once, without interrupting the exposition by any alien controversial matter. For the most part, it must find its evidence in its perfect congruity with all the established facts of the science.

CHAPTER II.

GENERAL LAW OF PROGRESSIVE COLOURATION.

IF the earliest petals were derived from flattened stamens, it would naturally follow that they would be for the most part yellow in colour, like the stamens from which they took their origin. How, then, did some of them afterwards come to be white, orange, red, purple, lilac, or blue? A few years ago, when the problem of the connection between flowers and insects still remained much in the state where Sprengel left it at the end of the last century, it would have seemed quite impossible to answer this question. But nowadays, after the full researches of Darwin, Wallace, Lubbock, and Hermann Müller into the subject, we can give a very satisfactory solution indeed. We now know, not only that the colours of flowers as a whole are intended to attract insects in general, but that certain colours are definitely intended to attract certain special kinds of insects. Thus, to take a few examples only out of hundreds that might be cited, the flowers which lay themselves out for fertilisation by miscellaneous small flies are almost always white; those which depend upon the beetles are frequently yellow; while those which specially bid for the favour of bees and butterflies are usually red, purple, lilac, or blue. Certain insects always visit one species of flower alone; and others pass from blossom to blossom of one kind only on a single day, though they may vary a little from kind to kind as the season advances, and one species replaces another. Müller, the most statistical of naturalists, has noticed that while bees form seventy-five per cent. of the insects visiting the very developed composites, they form only fourteen per cent. of those visiting umbelliferous plants, which have, as a rule, open but by no means showy white flowers. Certain blossoms which lay themselves out to attract wasps are, as he quaintly puts it, "obviously adapted to a less æsthetically cultivated circle of visitors." And some livid red flowers actually resemble in their colour and odour decaying raw meat, thus inducing bluebottle flies to visit them and so carry their pollen from head to head.

Down to the minutest distinctions between species, this correlation of flowers to the tastes of their particular guests seems to hold good. Hermann Müller notes that the common *Galium* of our heaths and hedges (*G. mollugo*) is white, and therefore visited by small flies; while the lady's bedstraw, its near relative (*G. verum*), is yellow, and owes its fertilisation to little beetles. Mr. H. O. Forbes counted on one occasion the visits he saw paid to the flowers on a single bank; and he found that a particular bumble-bee sucked the honey of thirty purple dead nettles in succession, passing over without notice all the other plants in the neighbourhood; two other species of bumble-bee and a cabbage-butterfly also patronised the same dead-nettles exclusively. Fritz Müller noticed a *Lantana* in South America which changes colour as its flowering advances; and he observed that each kind of butterfly which visited it stuck rigidly to its own favourite colour, waiting to pay its addresses until that colour appeared. Mr. Darwin cut off the petals of a lobelia and found that the hive-bees never went near it, though they were very busy with the surrounding flowers. But perhaps Sir John Lubbock's latest experiments on bees are the most conclusive of all. He had long ago convinced himself, by trials with honey placed on slips of glass above yellow, pink, or blue paper, that bees could discriminate the different colours; and he has now shown in the same way that they display a marked preference for blue over all other hues. The fact is, blue flowers are, as a rule, specialised for fertilisation by bees, and bees therefore prefer this colour; while conversely the flowers have at the same time become blue because that was the colour which the bees prefer. As in most other cases, the adaptation must have gone on *pari passu* on both sides. As the bee-flowers grew bluer, the bees must have grown fonder and fonder of blue; and as they grew fonder of blue, they must have more and more constantly preferred the bluest flowers.

We thus see how the special tastes of insects may have become the selective agency for developing white, pink, red, purple, and blue petals from the original yellow ones. But before they could exercise such a selective action, the petals must themselves have shown some tendency to vary in certain fixed directions. How could such an original tendency arise? For, of course, if the insects never saw any pink, purple, or blue petals, they could not specially favour and select them; so that we are as yet hardly nearer the solution of the problem than ever.

Here Mr. Sorby, who has chemically studied the colouring matter of leaves and flowers far more deeply than any other investigator, supplies us with a useful hint. He tells us that the various pigments of bright petals are already contained in the ordinary tissues of the plant, whose juices only need to be slightly modified in chemical constitution in order to make them into the blues, pinks, and purples with which we are so familiar. "The coloured substances in the petals," he says, "are in many cases exactly the same as those in the foliage from which chlorophyll has disappeared; so that the petals are often exactly like leaves which have turned yellow and red in autumn, or the very yellow or red leaves of early spring." "The colour of many crimson, pink, and red flowers is due to the development of substances belonging to the erythrophyll group, and not unfrequently to exactly the same kind as that so often found in leaves. The facts seem to indicate that these various substances may be due to an alteration of the normal constituents of leaves. So far as I have been able to ascertain, their development seems as if related to extra oxidisation, modified by light and other varying conditions not yet understood."

The different hues assumed by petals are all thus, as it were, laid up beforehand in the tissues of the plant, ready to be brought out at a moment's notice. And all flowers, as we know, easily sport a little in colour. But the question is, do their changes tend to follow any regular and definite order? Is there any reason to believe that the modification runs from any one colour toward any other? Apparently there is. The general conclusion to be set forth in this work is the statement of such a tendency. All flowers, it would seem, were in their earliest form yellow; then some of them became white; after that, a few of them grew to be red or purple; and finally, a comparatively small number acquired various shades of lilac, mauve, violet, or blue. So that, if this principle be true, such a flower as the harebell will represent one of the most highly-developed lines of descent; and its ancestors will have passed successively through all the intermediate stages. Let us see what grounds can be given for such a belief.

Some hints of a progressive law in the direction of a colour-change from yellow to blue are sometimes afforded us even by the successive stages of a single flower. For example, one of our common little English forget-me-nots, *Myosotis versicolor*, is pale yellow when it first opens; but as it grows older, it becomes faintly pinkish, and ends by being blue like the others of its race. Now, this sort of colour-change is by no means uncommon; and in almost all known cases it is always in the same direction, from yellow or white, through pink, orange, or red, to purple or blue. For example, one of the wall-flowers, *Cheiranthus chamæleo*, has at first a whitish flower, then a citron-yellow, and finally emerges into red or violet. The petals of *Stylidium fruticosum* are pale yellow to begin with, and afterwards become light rose-coloured. An evening primrose, *Œnothera tetraptera*, has white flowers in its first stage and red ones at a later period of development. *Cobæa scandens* goes from white to violet; *Hibiscus mutabilis* from white, through flesh-coloured, to red. The common Virginia stock of our gardens (*Malcolmia*) often opens of a pale yellowish green; then becomes faintly pink; afterwards deepens into bright red; and fades away at last into mauve or blue. Fritz Müller's *Lantana* is yellow on its first day, orange on the second, and purple on the third. The whole family of *Boraginaceæ* begin by being pink and end with being blue. The garden convolvulus opens a blushing white and passes into full purple. In all these and many other cases the general direction of the changes is the same. They are usually set down as due to varying degrees of oxidation in the pigmentary matter.

If this be so, there is a good reason why bees should be specially fond of blue, and why blue flowers should be specially adapted for fertilisation by their aid. For Mr. A. R. Wallace has shown that colour is most apt to appear or to vary in those parts of plants or animals which have undergone the highest amount of modification. The markings of the peacock and the argus pheasant come out upon their immensely developed secondary tail-feathers or wing-plumes; the metallic hues of sun-birds and humming-birds show themselves upon their highly-specialised crests, gorgets, or lappets. It is the same with the hackles of fowls, the head-ornaments of fruit pigeons, and the bills of toucans. The most exquisite colours in the insect world are those which are developed on the greatly expanded and delicately-feathered wings of butterflies; and the eye-spots which adorn a few species are usually found on their very highly modified swallow-tail appendages. So, too, with flowers; those which have undergone most modification have their colours most profoundly altered. In this way, we may put it down as a general rule (to be tested hereafter) that the least developed flowers are usually yellow or white; those which have undergone a little more modification are usually pink or red; and those which have been most highly specialised of any are usually purple, lilac, or blue. Absolute deep ultramarine probably marks the highest level of all.

On the other hand, Mr. Wallace's principle also explains why the bees and butterflies should prefer these specialised colours to all others, and should therefore select the flowers which display them by preference over any less developed types. For bees and butterflies are the most highly adapted of all insects to honey-seeking and flower-feeding. They have themselves on their side undergone the largest amount of specialisation for that particular function. And if the more specialised and modified flowers, which gradually fitted their forms and the position of their honey-glands to the forms of the bees or butterflies, showed a natural tendency to pass from yellow through pink and red to purple and blue, it would follow that the insects which were being evolved side by side with them, and which were aiding at the same time in their evolution, would grow to recognise these developed colours as the visible symbols of those flowers from which they could obtain the largest amount of honey with the least possible trouble. Thus it would finally result that the ordinary unspecialised flowers, which depended upon small insect riff-raff, would be mostly left yellow or white; those which appealed to rather higher insects would become pink or red; and those which laid themselves out for bees and butterflies, the aristocrats of the arthropodous world, would grow for the most part to be purple or blue.

Now, this is very much what we actually find to be the case in nature. The simplest and earliest flowers are those with regular, symmetrical, open cups, like the *Ranunculus* genus, the *Potentillas*, and the *Alsineæ*, or chickweeds, which can be visited by any insects whatsoever; and these are in large part yellow or white. A little higher are flowers like the campions or *Sileneæ*, and the stocks (*Matthiola*), with more or less closed cups, whose honey can only be reached by more specialised insects; and these are oftener pink or reddish. More profoundly modified are those irregular one-sided flowers, like the violets, peas, and orchids, which have assumed special shapes to accommodate bees or other specific honey-seekers; and these are often purple and not unfrequently blue. Highly specialised in another way are the flowers like harebells (*Campanula*), scabious (*Dipsaceæ*), and heaths (*Ericaceæ*), whose petals have all coalesced into a tubular corolla ; and these might almost be said to be usually purple or blue. And, finally, highest of all are the flowers like labiates (rosemary, *Salvia*, &c.) and speedwells (*Veronica*), whose tubular corolla has been turned to one side, thus combining the united petals with the irregular shape ; and these are almost invariably purple or blue.

We shall proceed to give a few selected examples from the families best represented in the British flora.

The very earliest types of angiospermous flowers now remaining are those in which the carpels still exist in a separate form, instead of being united into a single compound ovary. Among Dicotyledons, the families, some of whose members best represent this primitive stage, are the *Rosaceæ* and *Ranunculaceæ;* among Monocotyledons, the *Alismaceæ*. We may conveniently begin with the first group.

Fig. 5.—Flower of cinquefoil (*Potentilla*). Primitive yellow.

The roses form a most instructive family. As a whole they are not very highly developed flowers, since all of them have simple, open, symmetrical blossoms, generally with five distinct petals. But of all the rose tribe, the *Potentilleæ*, or cinquefoil group, including our common English silver-weed, seem to make up the most central, simple, and primitive members (Fig. 5). They are chiefly low, creeping weeds, and their flowers are of the earliest symmetrical pattern, without any specialisation of form, or any peculiar adaptation to insect visitors. Now, among the potentilla group, nearly all the blossoms have yellow petals, and also the filaments of the stamens yellow, as is likewise the case with the other early allied forms, such as agrimony (*Agrimonia Eupatoria*) and herb-bennet (*Geum urbanum*). Among our common yellow species are *Potentilla reptans* (cinquefoil), *P. tormentilla*, *P. argentea*, *P. verna*, *P. fruticosa*, and *P. anserina*. Almost the only white potentillas in England are the barren strawberry (*P. fragariastrum*) and the true strawberry (*Fragaria vesca*), which have, in many ways, diverged more than any other species from the norma of the race. Water-avens (*Geum rivale*), however, a close relative of herb-bennet, has a dusky purplish tinge; and Sir John Lubbock notes that it secretes honey, and is far oftener visited by insects than its kinsman. The bramble tribe (*Rubeæ*), including the blackberry (Fig. 6), raspberry, and dewberry, have much larger flowers than the potentillas, and are very greatly frequented by winged visitors. Their petals are usually pure white, often with a pinky tinge, especially on big, well-grown blossoms. But there is one low, little-developed member of the blackberry group, the *Rubus saxatilis*, or stone-bramble, with narrow, inconspicuous petals of a greenish-yellow, merging into dirty white; and this humble form seems to preserve for us the transitional stage from the yellow potentilla to the true white brambles. One step higher, the cherries and apples (though genetically unconnected), have very large and expanded petals, white toward the centre, but blushing at the edges into rosy pink or bright red (Fig. 7). We shall see hereafter

LAW OF PROGRESSIVE COLOURATION. 27

that new colours always make their appearance at the outer side of the petal, while the base usually retains its primitive colouration. For the present, this prin-

FIG. 6 —Vertical section of bramble-flower (*Rubus*). White.

ciple must be accepted on trust. Finally, the true roses (Fig. 8), whose flowers are the most developed of all, have usually broad pink petals (like those of our own

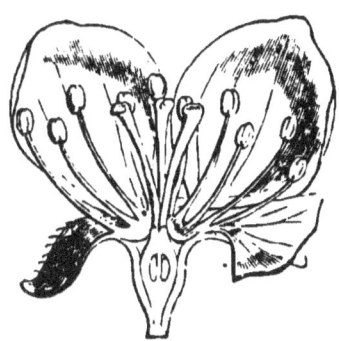

FIG. 7.—Vertical section of apple-blossom (*Pyrus malus*). Pinky white.

dog-rose, *Rosa canina, R. villosa, R. rubiginosa*, &c.), which, in some still bigger exotic species, become crimson or damask of the deepest dye. They are more sought after by insects than any others of their family.

Now, if we look closely at these facts, we see that they have several interesting implications. The yellow potentillas have the very simplest arrangement of the carpels in the whole family, and their fruit is of the most primitive character, consisting only of little dry separate nuts. They have altered very little from their primitive type. Accordingly, almost all the genus is yellow; a very few members only are white; and these in their habits so far vary from the rest that

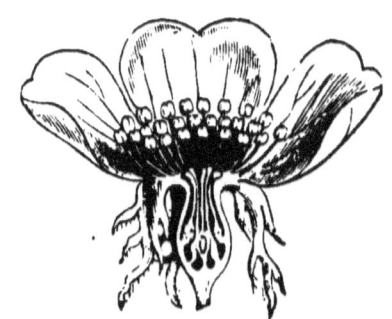

FIG. 8.—Vertical section of dog-rose (*Rosa*). Pink.

they have very erect flowers, and three leaflets instead of five or more to each leaf. One of them, the strawberry, shows still further marks of special differentiation, in that it has acquired a soft, pulpy, red fruit, produced by the swelling of the receptacle, and adapted to a safer mode of dispersal by the aid of birds. This group, however, including *Geum*, cannot claim to be considered the earliest ancestral form of the roses, because of its double calyx, which is not shared by other members of the family, as it would be if it had belonged to the actual common ancestor. In that respect, agrimony more nearly represents the primitive form, though its tall habit and large spikes of flowers show that it also has undergone a good deal of modification. Nevertheless, the yellow members of the potentilla group, in their low creeping habit, their want of woodiness, and their simple fruit, certainly remain very nearly at the primitive ancestral stage, and may be regarded as very early types of flowers indeed. It is only among handsome and showy exotic forms, which have undergone a good deal more modification, that we get brilliant red-flowered species like the East Indian *P. nepalensis* and *P. atropurpurea*.

But as soon as the plants rise a little in the scale, and the flowers grow larger, we get a general tendency towards white and pink blossoms. Thus the *Pruneæ* have diverged from the central stock of the rose family in one direction, and the *Pomeæ* and *Roseæ* in another; but both alike begin at once to assume white petals; and as they lay themselves out more and more distinctly for insect aid, the white passes gradually into pink and rose-colour. To trace the gradations throughout, we see that the *Rubeæ*, or brambles, are for the most part woody shrubs instead of being mere green herbs, and they have almost all whitish blossoms instead of yellow ones; but their carpels still remain quite distinct, and they seldom rise to the third stage of pinkiness; when they do it is generally just as they are fading, and we may lay it down as a common principle that the fading colours of less developed petals often answer to the normal colours of more developed. In the *Pruneæ*, again, the development has gone much further, for here most of the species are trees or hard shrubs, and the number of carpels is reduced to one. They have a succulent fruit—a drupe, the highest type—and though the flower contains two ovules, the ripe plum has only one seed, the other having become abortive. All these are marks of high evolution: indeed, in most respects the *Pruneæ* stand at the very head of the rose family; but the petals are seldom very expanded, and so, though they are usually deeply tinged with pink in the cherry (*Prunus cerasus*), and still more so in larger exotic blossoms, like the almond, the peach, and the nectarine, they seldom reach the stage of red. Our own sloe (*P. communis*) has smallish white flowers, as has also the Portugal laurel (*P. lusitanicus*). In these plants, in fact, higher development has not largely taken the direction of increased attraction for insect fertilizers; it has mainly concentrated itself upon the fruit, and the devices for its dispersal by birds or mammals. In the *Roseæ*, on the other hand, though the fruit is less highly modified, the methods for ensuring insect fertilisation are carried much further. There are several carpels, but they are inclosed within the tube of the calyx, and the petals are very much enlarged indeed, while in some species the styles are united in a column. As regards insect-attraction, indeed, the roses are the most advanced members of the family, and it is here, accordingly, that we get the highest types of colouration. Most of them are at least pink, and many are deep red or crimson. Among the *Pomeæ*, we find an intermediate type (as regards the flowers alone) between *Roseæ* and *Pruneæ*; the petals are usually bigger and pinker than those of the plums; not so big or so pink as those of the true roses. This interesting series exhibits very beautifully the importance as regards colouration of mere expansion in the petals. Taking them as a whole we may say that the smallest petals in the rose family are generally yellow; the next in size are generally white; the third in order are generally pink; and the largest are generally rose-coloured or crimson.

At the same time, the roses as a whole, being a relatively simple family, with regular symmetrical flowers of the separate or polypetalous type, have never risen to the stage of producing blue petals. That, probably, is why our florists cannot turn out a blue rose. It is easy enough to make roses or any other blossoms vary within their own natural limits, revert to any earlier form or colour through which they have previously passed; but it is difficult or impossible to make them take a step which they have never yet naturally taken. Hence florists generally find the most developed flowers are also the most variable and plastic in colour; and hence, too, we can get red, pink, white, straw-coloured, or yellow roses, but not blue ones. This would seem to be the historical truth underlying De Candolle's division of flowers into a xanthic and cyanic series. Of course, there is nothing to prevent florists from developing a blue rose in the same way as the insects would do it, by gradually selecting and preserving the most bluish or slate-coloured among their pink or crimson kinds. But it would appear from the comparative rarity of blue flowers in nature that the spontaneous variations which make towards blue are far less frequent than those which make towards pink, red, purple, or orange.

There is one small set of rosaceous plants which exhibit green flowers, such as the genera *Alchemilla* and *Poterium*. When we come to consider the subject of degeneration, however, we shall see that these are not really primitive blossoms, but very degraded and altered types. For the present, it must suffice to point out that they have lost some of their sepals, all their petals, and many of their carpels ; and that they cannot therefore be regarded in any way as representatives of the central primordial stock from which the roses are originally derived. This place certainly belongs rather to *Potentilla, Agrimonia*, and some allied exotic types, with simple regular yellow blossoms.

Even more primitive in type than the *Rosaceæ* are the lowest members of the *Ranunculaceæ*, or buttercup family, which perhaps best of all preserve for us the original features of the early dicotyledonous flowers. The family is also more interesting than that of the roses because it contains greater diversities of development, and accordingly covers a wider range of colour, its petals varying from yellow to every shade of crimson, purple, and blue. The simplest and least differentiated members of the group are the common meadow buttercups (Fig. 9), forming the genus *Ranunculus*, which, as everybody knows, have five open petals of a brilliant golden hue. Nowhere else is the exact accordance in tint between stamens and petals more noticeable than in these flowers. The colour of the filaments is exactly the same as that of the petals; and the latter are simply the former a little expanded and deprived of their anthers. We have several English meadow species, all with separate carpels, and all very primitive in organization, such as *R. acris* (the central form), *R. bulbosus, R. repens, R. flammula, R. sceleratus, R. auricomus, R. philonotis*, &c. In the lesser celandine or pilewort, *R. ficaria*, there is a slight divergence from the ordinary habit of the genus, in that the petals, instead of being five in number, are eight or nine, while the sepals are only three; and this divergence is accompanied by two slight variations in colour: the outside of the petals tends to become slightly reddish or purplish, and the flowers fade

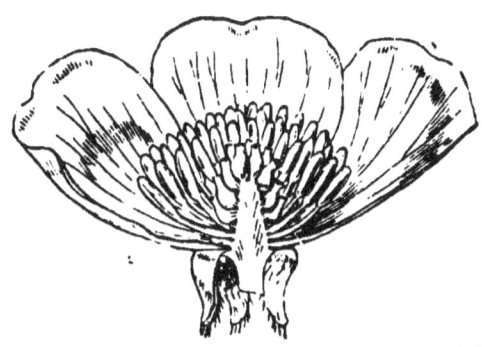

FIG. 9.—Vertical section of buttercup (*Ranunculus acris*); primitive yellow.

white, much more distinctly than in most other species of the genus.

There are two kinds of buttercup in England, however, which show us the transition from yellow to white actually taking place under our very eyes. These are the water-crowfoot, *R. aquatilis* (Fig. 9*a*), and its close ally the ivy-leaved crowfoot, *R. hederaceus*, whose petals are still faintly yellow toward the centre, but fade away into primrose and white as they approach the edge. We have already noticed that new colours usually appear at the outside, while the claw or base

D

of the petal retains its original hue; and this law is strikingly illustrated in these two crowfoots. It is remarkable, too, that in this respect they closely resemble the half-faded flowers of the lesser celandine, which become white from the edge inward as they die. The petals also similarly vary in number, though to a less extent. White flowers of the same type as those of water-crowfoot are very common among aquatic plants of like habit, and they seem to be especially adapted to water-side insects.

Fig. 9a.—Flower of water crowfoot (*Ranunculus aquatilis*); white, with yellow claws.

In many *Ranunculaceæ* there is a great tendency for the sepals to become petaloid, and this peculiarity is very marked in *Caltha palustris*, the marsh-marigold, which has no petals, but bright yellow sepals, so that it looks at first sight exactly like a very large buttercup.

The clematis and anemone, which are more highly developed, have white sepals (for the petals here also are suppressed), even in our English species; and exotic kinds varying from pink to purple are cultivated in our flower-gardens.

It is among the higher ranunculaceous plants, however, that we get the fullest and richest colouration. Columbines (*Aquilegia*) are very specialised forms of the buttercup type (Fig. 10). Both sepals and petals

Fig. 10.—Flower of columbine (*Aquilegia vulgaris*), with petals produced into honey-bearing spurs; purple or blue.

are brightly coloured, while the former organs are produced above into long, bow-shaped spurs (Fig. 11), each of which secretes a drop of honey. The carpels are also reduced to five, the regularity of number being itself a common mark of advance in organization. Various columbines accordingly range from red to purple and dark blue. Our English species, *A. vulgaris*, is blue or dull purple, though it readily reverts to white or red in cultivated varieties. Even the columbine, however, though so highly specialised, is not bilaterally but circularly symmetrical. This last and highest mode of adaptation to insect visits is found in larkspur (*Delphinium ajacis*), and still more developed in the curious monkshood (*Aconitum napellus*, Fig. 12).

FIG. 11.—Petal of columbine produced into a honey-bearing spur.

Now larkspur is usually blue, though white or red blossoms sometimes occur by reversion; while monkshood is one of the deepest blue flowers we possess. Both show very high marks of special adaptation; for besides their bilateral form, *Delphinium* has the number of carpels reduced to one, the calyx coloured and deeply spurred, and three of the petals abortive; while *Aconitum* has the carpels reduced to three and partially united into a compound ovary, the upper sepals altered into a curious coloured hood or helmet, and the petals considerably modified (Fig. 13). All these very complex arrangements are defintely correlated with the visits of insects, for the two highly abnormal petals under the helmet of the monkshood produce honey, as do also the two long petals within the spur of the larkspur. Both flowers are also specially adapted to the very highest class of insect visitors.

FIG. 12.—Flowers of monkshood (*Aconitum napellus*), dark blue.

Aconitum is chiefly fertilized by bees; and Sir John Lubbock observes that "*Anthophora pilipes* and *Bombus hortorum* are the only two North European insects which have a proboscis long enough to reach to the end of the spur of *Delphinium elatum*. *A.*

pilipes, however, is a spring insect, and has already disappeared before the *Delphinium* comes into flower, so that it appears to depend for its fertilisation entirely on *Bombus hortorum*."

Thus within the limits of the *Ranunculaceæ* we get every gradation in colouring, from the very simple, open, yellow buttercups, through the white water

FIG. 13.— Petals of monkshood, concealed by sepals, and produced into honey-bearing sacs.

crowfoots, the red adonis, the scarlet pæony, and the purple columbine, to the very irregular blue larkspur, and the extremely complex ultramarine monkshood. In this family it may be noted, too, that increase of adaptation to insect visits is shown rather by peculiarities of shape and arrangement than by mere increased size of petals, as among the roses.

Observe also that every advance either in insect

fertilization or in special adaptation for dispersal of seeds results in a lessening of the number of carpels or of seeds. The plant does not need to produce so many when all are fairly sure of arriving at maturity and being dispersed.

Flowers in which the carpels have arranged themselves in a circle around a common axis, like the *Geraniaceæ* and *Malvaceæ*, thereby show themselves to be more highly modified than flowers in which all the carpels are quite separate and scattered, like the simpler *Rosaceæ* and *Ranunculaceæ*. Still more do families such as the *Caryophyllaceæ*, or pinks, in which all the five primitive carpels have completely coalesced into a single five-celled ovary. Accordingly, it is not remarkable that the pinks should never be yellow. On the other hand, this family has no very specialised members, like the larkspur and the monkshood, and therefore it very rarely produces bluish or purplish flowers. Pinks, in fact, do not display so wide a range in either direction as *Ranunculaceæ*. They begin as high up as white, and hardly get any higher than red or carnation. They are divisible into two sub-families, *Alsineæ* and *Sileneæ*. The *Alsineæ* have the sepals free, the blossoms widely expanded, and no special adaptations for insect fertilization (Fig. 14). They include all the small undeveloped field species, such as the chickweeds (*Stellaria media, Arenaria trinervis, Cerastium vulgatum*, &c.), stitchworts (*Stellaria holostea*, &c.), and cornspurries (*Spergula arvensis*), which have open flowers of a very primitive character; and almost all of them are white. These are fertilized by miscellaneous small flies. The *Sileneæ*, on the other hand, including the large-flowered types such as the campions (Fig. 15) and true pinks, have a tubular calyx, formed by the coalescence of the five sepals, and the expanded petals are raised on long claws; which makes their honey, inclosed in the tube, accessible only to the higher insects. Most of them also display special adaptations for a better class of insect fertilization in the way of fringes or crowns on the petals. These more profoundly modified kinds are

FIG. 14.—Flowers of chickweed (*Stellaria*); white.

generally pink or red. For example, in the most advanced British genus, *Dianthus*, which has usually vandyked edges to the petals, our four English species are all brightly coloured, *D. armeria*, the Deptford pink, being red with dark spots, *D. prolifer* purplish red, *D. deltoides*, the maiden pink, rosy spotted with white, and *D. cæsius*, the Cheddar pink, bright rose-coloured. It is much the same with the allied genus *Lychnis*.

Our own beautiful purple English corn-cockle (*L. githago*), is a highly developed campion, so specialised that only butterflies can reach its honey with their long tongues, as the nectaries are situated at the bottom of the tube. Two other species of campion, however, show us interestingly the way in which variations of colour may occur in a retrograde direction even among highly evolved forms.

FIG. 15.—Flower of night campion (*Lychnis vespertina*); white.

One of them, the day lychnis, (*L. diurna*), has red, scentless flowers, opening in the morning, and it is chiefly fertilized by diurnal butterflies. But its descendant, the night lychnis (*L. vespertina*), has taken to fertilization by means of moths; and as moths can only see white flowers it has become white (Fig. 15), and has acquired a faint perfume as an extra attraction. Still, the change has not yet become fully organised in the species, for one may often find a night lychnis at the present time which is only pale pink, instead of being pure white.

Sir John Lubbock remarks of the *Caryophyllaceæ* that "the order presents us with an interesting series commencing with open-flowered species, the honey of which is accessible even to beetles, and short-tongued flies, through those which are adapted to certain flies (Rhingia) and Bees; to the species of *Dianthus, Saponaria*, and *Lychnis Githago*, the honey of which is accessible to Lepidoptera only." It is a curious fact that in just the same progression the flowers pass gradually from small white inconspicuous petals to large and deeply coloured red or purple ones.

The *Cistaceæ* are another family of simple flowers, with the carpels united, but otherwise very primitive in form. Their petals usually spread around the ovary in a regular discoid form; and the earliest members only differ essentially from *Potentilla* in the union of their carpels into a single imperfectly three-celled capsule. Our English genus, *Helianthemum* or rock-rose, comprises some of the smallest and simplest forms, with yellow petals, and very like *Potentilla* in general appearance. One species, however, *H. polifolium* (a mere slight variation on the yellow *H. vulgare*), has white flowers. The larger South European forms, which make up the genus *Cistus*, have much more expanded petals, and these are usually white, pinkish, or rose-coloured. One Mediterranean species has a yellow centre with white edges: another closely allied to it, has a white centre with pink edges. Here, as in the roses, mere increase in size (coupled of course with special insect selection) seems to have effected the progressive modification of the pigmentary matter.

The *Papaveraceæ* or poppies show us somewhat similar results. Many of the less developed forms, with small petals, are yellow. For example, the celandine, *Chelidonium majus*, has a very simple ovary and comparatively inconspicuous flowers: and its petals are of just the same primitive golden yellow as those of the buttercups, the potentillas, and the rock-roses. *Glaucium luteum*, another little-developed form, is also yellow. So are the Californian *Eschscholtzias* of our gardens. But in the field poppies, *Papaver rhœas, P. dubium, P. hybridum*, &c., which have extremely large and expanded petals, together with a highly modified compound ovary, bright scarlet is the prevailing colour, though pale red and white also occur. The still larger garden poppy, *P. somniferum*, is bluish white, with a purple base to the petals.

The *Cruciferæ* are a family which display a good deal of variety of colouration, though not so largely within the limits of our British species. The most primitive and simple forms have yellow flowers, as in the case of the cabbage genus (*Brassica*) including charlock, mustard, and turnip; the rockets (*Barbarea* and *Sisymbrium*); and the gold-of-pleasure (*Camelina sativa*). Most of these are dry-field weeds, and they have open little-developed blossoms. Their petals usually fade white. In the genus *Nasturtium* or watercress we have four species, three of which are yellow, while one is white. In treacle-mustard (*Erysimum*), the yellow is very pale, and the petals often become almost white. Just above these earliest forms come the common small white crucifers like *Cardamine hirsuta, Cochlearia officinalis,* and *Capsella bursa-pastoris.* Many of these are little if at all superior in organization to the yellow species, and some of them (as we shall see hereafter) are evidently degenerate weeds of cultivation. But such flowers as *Alyssum maritimum,* with its sweet scent, its abundant honey, its reduced number of seeds, and its conspicuous, spreading milk-white petals, are certainly more developed than small yellow species like *Alyssum calycinum.* Even more remarkably is this the case in the genus *Iberis* or candytuft, which has become slightly irregular, by the two adjoining exterior petals growing larger than the interior ones. They thus form very conspicuous heads of bloom, obviously adapted to higher insect fertilisation. Accordingly, they are usually white, like our British species, *I. amara;* while some of the larger exotic species are a pretty pink in hue. The genus *Cardamine* supplies us with like instances. Here the smaller species have white flowers, and so has the large *C. amara.* But in *C. pratensis,* the cuckoo-flower, they are usually tinged with a pinkish purple, which often fades deep mauve; and in some showy exotic species the flowers are a rich pink. So with *Arabis:* our small English kinds are white; *A. petræa,* with larger petals, is often slightly purplish, and some handsome exotics are a vivid purple. In *Hesperis* we get a further degree of modification in that the petals are raised on rather long claws; and the flowers (represented in England by *H. matronalis,* the dame's-violet) are a fine purple and possess a powerful perfume. Closely allied is the Virginia stock of our gardens, (*Malcolmia*) which varies from pale pink to mauve : its calyx has become tubular. Yellow blossoms occasionally occur in this genus. But the highest of all our crucifers are contained in the genera *Matthiola* and *Cheiranthus*, which have large spreading petals on long erect claws, besides often being sweet scented. The common stock (*M. incana*) is purple, reddish, or even violet ; our other British species, *M. sinuata*, is pale lilac ; and no member of the genus is ever yellow. The wallflower (*Cheiranthus cheiri*) is rich orange or red, sometimes yellow : its colour, however, differs widely from the primitive golden yellow of the charlocks or buttercups ; and it will receive further attention hereafter.

There is one special (perhaps artificial) tribe of crucifers, the *Lomentosæ*, which display specially high modification in the pod or fruit; and these deserve separate treatment. Yellow flowers are here very rare ; but one English species, *Isatis tinctoria*, the dyer's woad, has small yellow petals. *Raphanus raphanistrum*, the wild radish, has usually in its seacoast form pale primrose blossoms, much larger than woad ; but inland they are oftener white with coloured veins, and sometimes even lilac. *Crambe maritima*, the seakale, a somewhat more developed type, is always white, never yellow ; and *Cakile maritima*, a still higher plant of the same tribe, has purple blossoms, much like those of a stock.

So much by way of illustration of the families with usually regular polypetalous flowers and free superior ovaries. The other families of this type not noticed here will receive attention in a later chapter. We may next pass on to the families of polypetalous flowers with usually irregular corollas, which represent of course a higher stage of development in adaptation to insect visits.

Of these, three good illustrative cases are included in the British flora. They are the *Polygalaceæ*, the *Violaceæ*, and the *Papilionaceæ*.

Polygala vulgaris, or milkwort, our only British representative of the first named family, is an extremely irregular flower, very minutely and remarkably modified for special insect fertilisation. It is usually a bright blue in colour, but it often reverts to pink, and not infrequently even to white. Two of the sepals are coloured, as well as the petals.

The *Violaceæ* or violets are a whole family of bilateral flowers, highly adapted to fertilisation by insects; and as a rule they are a deep blue in colour. This is the case with four of our British species, *Viola odorata*, *V. canina*, *V. hirta*, and *V. palustris*. Here, too, however, white varieties easily arise by reversion; while one member of the group, the common pansy, *V. tricolor*, is perhaps the most variable flower in all nature. This case, again, will receive further attention when we come to consider the subject of variegation and of reversion or retrogression.

The *Papilionaceæ* or peaflowers are closely related to the roses, but differ conspicuously in their bilateral form. The lower and smaller species, such as the medick, lotus, and lady's fingers, are usually yellow, though often reddish outside. So also are broom and gorse. Among the more specialised clovers, some of which are fertilised by bees alone, white, red, and purple predominate. Even with the smaller and earlier types, the most developed species, like lucerne, are likewise purple or blue. But in the largest and most advanced types, the peas, beans, vetches, and scarlet runners, we get much brighter and deeper colours, often with more or less tinge of blue. In the sweet-peas and many others, the standard frequently differs in hue from the keel or the wings— a still further advance in heterogeneity of colouration. Lupines, sainfoin, everlasting pea, and wistaria are highly evolved members of the same family, in which purple, lilac, mauve, or blue tints become distinctly pronounced. The colouration of the *Papilionaceæ*, however, does not as a whole illustrate the general law so well as that of many other groups.

When we pass on to the *Corolliflorœ*, or flowers in which the originally separate petals have coalesced into a single united tube, we meet with much more striking results.

Here, where the very shape at once betokens high modification, yellow is a comparatively rare colour (especially as a ground-tone, though it often comes out in spots or patches), while purple and blue, so rare elsewhere, become almost the rule.

The family of *Campanulaceæ*, or bluebells, forms an excellent example. Its flowers are usually blue or white, and the greater number of them, like the harebell (*Campanula rotundifolia*) and the Canterbury bell (*C. media*), are deep blue (Fig. 16). We have nine British species of the genus, varying from pale sky-blue to ultramarine and purplish cobalt, with an occasional relapse to white. Rampion and sheep's bit, also blue, are clustered heads of similar blossoms. The little blue lobelia of our borders, which is bilateral as well as tubular, belongs to a closely-related tribe. One of our British species, *Lobelia Dortmanna*, is sky-blue; the other, *L. urens*, is a dingy purple. Not far from them are the *Dipsaceæ*, including the lilac scabious, the blue devil's bit, and the mauve teasel. Amongst

Fig. 16.—Flower of harebell (*Campanula*); bright blue.

all these very highly-evolved groups blue distinctly forms the prevalent colour.

In the great family of the *Ericaceæ*, or heaths, which is highly adapted to insect fertilisation, more particularly by bees, purple and rose are the prevailing tints, so much so that, as we all have noticed a hundred times over, they often colour whole tracts of hillside together. In all probability there are no really yellow heaths. The bell-shaped blossoms mark at once the position of the heaths with reference to insects; and the order, according to Mr. Bentham, supplies us with more ornamental plants than any other in the whole world. Among our British species, in the less developed forms, like *Vaccinium, Arbutus,* and *Andromeda,* the flowers are usually white, flesh-coloured, pinkish, or reddish. The highly developed *Ericæ,* on the other hand, are mostly purple or deep red. *E. vulgaris* has the calyx as well as the corolla coloured with a mauve variety of pink. *Menziesia cærulea* is a deep purplish blue. *Monotropa* alone, a very degraded leafless saprophyte form, has greenish-yellow or pale brown free petals.

The *Boraginaceæ* are another very advanced family of *Corolliflora,* and they are blue almost without exception. They have usually highly-modified flowers, with a tube below and spreading lobes above; in addition to which most of the species possess remarkable and strongly-developed appendages to the corolla, in the way of teeth, crowns, hairs, scales, parapets or valves. Of the common British species alone, the forget-me-nots (*Myosotis*) are clear sky-blue with a yellow eye; the viper's bugloss (*Echium vulgare*) is at first reddish purple, and afterwards a deep blue; the lungwort (*Pulmonaria officinalis*) is also dark blue; and so are the two alkanets (*Anchusa*), the true bugloss (*Lycopsis*), the madwort (*Asperugo*), and the familiar borage (*Borago officinalis*), used to flavour claret-cup; though all of them by reversion occasionally produce purple or white flowers. Houndstongue (*Cynoglossum officinale*) is purple-red, and most of the other species vary between purple and blue; indeed, throughout the family most flowers are red at first and blue as they mature. The purplish-red of the less advanced species exactly answers to the immature colouring of the more advanced, which are blue in their full-blown stage. Of these, borage at least is habitually fertilised by bees, and the same is partially true of many of the other species. All of them are adapted to a high class of insect visitors.

Other families of regular *Corolliflorœ* must be glanced at more briefly. Among the *Gentianaceœ*, the less advanced types, like the simple *Chlora perfoliata* and *Limnanthemum nymphœoides*, are yellow, perhaps by reversion; but *Menyanthes trifoliata*, a slightly more developed ally of *Limnanthemum*, has white blossoms, tinged outside with red; *Erythrœa centaurium*, with a divided calyx and the cells of the ovary imperfectly united, is red; and the true gentians, *Gentiana verna*, *G. campestris*, *G. nivalis*, &c., with a tubular calyx, long throat, and sometimes fringed hairs to the tube, are bright blue. In *Apocynaceœ*, we have the highly developed periwinkles, *Vinca major* and *V. minor*, normally blue, though pink and white varieties or species are also cultivated. In *Plumbagineœ* we have the bluish purple sea-lavender (*Statice Limonium*) and the pink thrift (*Armeria vulgaris*). Other families with special peculiarities will receive notice later on.

It is necessary, however, here briefly to refer to the great family of *Compositœ*, some of whose peculiarities can only properly be considered when we come to inquire into the phenomena of relapse and retrogression. Nevertheless, even at the present stage of our inquiry, the composites afford some excellent evidence. In certain ways they may be regarded as the very highest race of flowering plants. Not only are their petals united into a tubular corolla, but their blossoms are compounded into large bunches or groups of a very showy and attractive sort. Each flower-head here consists of a number of small florets, crowded together so as to resemble a single blossom. So far as our present purpose is concerned, they fall naturally into three groups—Jussieu's old-fashioned sub-orders of *Ligulatæ*, *Cynaroideæ*, and *Corymbiferæ*, which are quite sufficient for all ordinary objects of botanical study. The first, or ligulate tribe, is that of the dandelions or hawkweeds, with open florets, fertilised, as a rule, by very small insects; and these are generally yellow, with only a very few divergent species. They will receive further notice hereafter. The second, or cynaroid tribe, is that of the thistle-heads, visited by an immense number of insects, including the bees; and these are almost all purple, while some highly-evolved species, like the corn-flower or blue-bottle (*Centaurea cyanus*, Fig. 17) and the true artichoke (*Cynara scolymus*), are bright blue. The third, or corymbiferous tribe, is that of the daisies and asters, with tubular central florets and long flattened outer rays; and these demand a closer examination here.

The central florets of the daisy tribe, as a rule, are bright golden; a fact which shows pretty certainly that they are descended from a common ancestor who was also yellow. Moreover, these yellow florets are bell-shaped, and each contains a pistil and five stamens, like any other perfect flower. But the outer florets are generally sterile; and instead of being

Fig. 17.—Flower of corn bluebottle (*Centaurea cyanus*); highest type of cynaroid composite; bright blue.

bell-shaped they are split down one side and unrolled, so as to form a long ray; while their corolla is at the same time much larger than that of the central blossoms (Fig. 18). In short, they are sterilised members of the compound flower-head, specially set apart for the work of display; and thus they stand to the entire flower-head in the same relation as petals do to the simple original flower. The analogy between the two is complete. Just as the petal is a specialised and sterilised stamen told off to do duty as an allurer of insects for the benefit of the whole flower, so the ray-floret is a specialised and sterilised blossom told off to do the self-same duty for the benefit

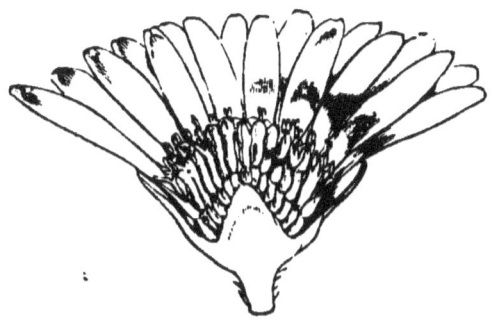

FIG. 18.—Vertical section of head of daisy (*Bellis perennis*); central florets, yellow; ray florets, white, tipped with pink.

of the group of tiny flowers which make up the composite flower-head.

Now, the earliest ray-florets would naturally be bright-yellow, like the tubular blossoms of the central disk from which they sprang. And to this day the ray-florets of the simplest corymbiferous types, such as the corn-marigold (*Chrysanthemum segetum*), the sun-flower (*Helianthus annuus*), and the ragwort (*Senecio jacobæa*), are yellow like the central flowers. In the camomile, however, the ox-eye daisy, and the may-weed (*Anthemis cotula, Chrysanthemum leucanthemum*, &c.), the rays have become white; and this,

I think, fairly establishes the fact that white is a higher development of colour than yellow; for the change must surely have been made in order to attract special insects. Certainly, such a differentiation of the flowers in a single head cannot be without a good purpose. In the true daisy, again (*Bellis perennis*), the white rays become tipped with pink (Fig. 18) which sometimes rises almost to rose-colour; and this stage is exactly analogous to that of apple-blossom, which similarly halts on the way from white petals to red. In our own asters (*A. tripolium*, &c.) and the Michaelmas daisies of America, we get a further advance to purple, lilac, and mauve, while both in these and in the chrysanthemums true shades of blue not infrequently appear. The *Cinerarias* of our gardeners are similar forms of highly-developed groundsels from the Canary Islands.

Tubular flowers with an irregular corolla are obviously higher in their mode of adaptation to insect visits than tubular flowers of the ordinary symmetrical type. Amongst them, the first place must be assigned to the *Labiates*—perhaps the most specialised of any so far as regards insect fertilisation. Not only are they deeply tubular, but they are very bilateral and irregular indeed, displaying more modification of form than almost any other flowers except the orchids. They mostly secrete abundant honey, and often possess highly aromatic perfumes. Moreover, they form geologically one of the latest families of flowering plants, specially developed in adaptation to bees and other highly-evolved honey-suckers. Almost all of them are purple or blue. Among the best known English species are thyme, mint, marjoram,

LAW OF PROGRESSIVE COLOURATION. 55

sage (Fig. 19), and basil, which it need hardly be said are great favourites with bees. Ground-ivy (*Nepeta glechoma*) is bright blue; catmint (*Nepeta cataria*), pale blue; *Prunella*, violet-purple; and common bugle (*Ajuga reptans*), blue or flesh-colour. Many of the others are purple or purplish. It must be added that in this family the flowers are very liable to vary within the limit of the same species; and red, white, or purple specimens are not uncommon in many of the normally blue kinds.

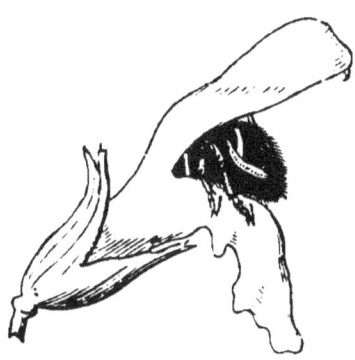

FIG. 19.—Flower of sage (*Salvia*) visited by bee; blue.

The *Scrophularineæ* and other allied irregular tubular families are mostly spotted, and so belong to a later stage of our inquiry; but even amongst this group, the *Veronica* genus has almost always pure blue flowers; foxglove (*Digitalis purpurea*) is purple; and most of the Broomrapes (*Orobanchaceæ*) are more or less bluish. Blue and lilac also appear abundantly in spots or stripes in many species of *Linaria*, in *Euphrasia*, and in other genera.

We have given so much consideration to the Dicotyledons that the relatively simple and homogeneous

Monocotyledons need not detain us long. Their colouration is as a whole both less complicated and less instructive. As a rule, sepals and petals are here petaloid and often indistinguishable.

The *Alismaceæ* answer very closely to the *Ranunculaceæ* as being in all probability the earliest surviving type of entomophilous Monocotyledons. Their arrangement is of course trinary, but they have similarly separate carpels, often numerous, surrounded by one, two, three, or many rows of stamens, and then by one row of three petals and one row of three sepals. All our English species, however, are white or rosy, instead of yellow. As they are marsh plants, they seem to have reached or passed the stage of *Ranunculus aquatilis*. One species, *Alisma plantago*, the water-plantain, however, still retains a yellow claw to the petals, though the limb is white or pale pink. So also does *Damasonium stellatum*. These two interesting plants present a remarkable analogy to the water-crowfoot.

Among monocotyledonous families with a united ovary, the *Liliaceæ* are probably the most primitive. Their simplest type in England is *Gagea lutea* (Fig. 20), a yellow lily looking extremely like a bunch of *Ranunculus Ficaria*. In *Lloydia serotina*, a closely allied but more developed form, the petals are white, with a yellow base, and three reddish lines. The wild tulip is likewise yellow. *Allium ursinum*, a somewhat higher type, is pure white. The fritillary (*Fritillaria Meleagris*), a large, handsome, bell-shaped flower, with separate petals converging into a campanulate form, and with a nectariferous cavity at their base (Fig. 21), is purple or red, chequered with lurid marks;

but it often reverts to white or even to a faint yellow. In *Scilla*, however, including our common wild hyacinth (*S. nutans*), the deep tubular flowers, composed of perianth pieces with long claws, are usually blue, rarely pink or white; while in *Hyacinthus* and *Muscari*, which have a united bell-shaped or globular blossom, formed by the coalescence of the sepals and petals, dark-blue and ultramarine are the prevalent

FIG. 20.—Flowers of simplest typical lily (*Gagea lutea*); primitive yellow.

tones. Meadow saffron (*Colchicum autumnale*), which has also a united tube and very deep underground ovary, is a fine reddish purple: its stamens secrete honey.

The *Irideæ* and *Amaryllideæ* are more advanced than the lilies, in that they possess inferior ovaries— in other words, their perianth tube has coalesced with the walls of the inclosed carpels. In many cases, especially in the more highly-developed species, their flowers are red, blue, or purple. *Trichonema Bulbocodium* is purplish-blue with a yellow centre. Our two native crocuses (*C. vernus* and *C. nudiflorus*) are also purple. *Sisyrinchium Bermudianum* is a delicate blue. *Gladiolus communis* is brilliant crimson. *Iris fœtidissima* (Fig. 22) is violet. Our own Amaryllids are white or primrose, but brilliant reds and purples,

Fig. 21.—Flower of fritillary (*Fritillaria Meleagris*); purple, spotted with white.

as well as highly-developed spotted types, are common amongst the cultivated exotics.

The *Orchidaceæ* stand at the head of the entomophilous Monocotyledons by virtue of their inferior ovary, their irregular flowers, and their extraordinary adaptations to insect fertilization. Purples are the prevailing ground-tones; but in the commonness of variegation and of specialized lines or spots of colour the Orchids answer closely to the *Scrophularineæ*

LAW OF PROGRESSIVE COLOURATION. 59

among Dicotyledons, and may therefore best be considered in the succeeding chapter.

This brief review of the chief families of English entomophilous flowers will probably have made clear the general truth of the law of progressive colouration here laid down. There are many exceptions and special peculiarities, some of which will be explained

FIG 22.—Flower of common flag (*Iris fœtidissima*); violet blue.

or accounted for in the sequel; but on the whole we may consider the following facts fairly proved :—

(1.) Most of the very simplest flowers are yellow.

(2.) Many of the simpler flowers in each family (except the highest) are apt to be yellow.

(3.) The more advanced members of very simple families are usually white or pink.

(4.) The simpler members of slightly advanced families are usually white or pink.

(5.) The most advanced members of all families are usually red, purple, or blue.

(6.) Almost all the members of the most advanced families are purple or blue.

(7.) The most advanced members of the most advanced families are almost always blue, unless spotted or variegated.

CHAPTER III.

VARIEGATION.

So far we have spoken for the most part only of what ladies would call self-colour, as though every flower were of one unvaried hue throughout. We must now add a few considerations on the subject of the spots and lines which so often variegate the petals in certain species. In this connection, again, Mr. Wallace's hint is full of meaning. Everywhere in nature, he points out, spots and eyes of colour appear on the most highly-modified parts, and this rule applies most noticeably to the case of petals. Simple regular flowers, like the buttercups and roses, hardly ever have any spots or lines; but in very modified forms like the labiates and the orchids they are extremely common. The scrophularineous family, to which the snap-dragon belongs, is one most specially adapted to insects, and even more irregular than that of the labiates; and here we find the most singular effects produced by dappling and mixture of colours. The simple yellow mullein, it is true, has few such spots or lines, nor have even many of the much higher blue veronicas; but in the snapdragons, the foxglove, the toadflax, the ivy-linaria, the eyebright, and the calceolarias, the intimate mixture of colours is very noticeable. In the allied tropical *Bignonias* and *Gloxinias* we see much the same distribution of hues. Many of the family are cultivated in gardens on account of their bizarre and fantastic shapes and colours. As to the orchids, it is hardly necessary to say anything about their wonderfully spotted and variegated flowers. Even in our small English kinds the dappling is extremely marked, especially upon the expanded and profoundly modified lower lip; but in the larger tropical varieties the patterns are often quaint and even startling in their extraordinary richness of fancy and apparent capriciousness of design. Mr. Darwin has shown that their adaptations to insects are more intimate and more marvellous than those of any other flowers whatsoever.

Structurally speaking, the spots and lines on petals seem to be the direct result of high modification; but functionally, as Sprengel long ago pointed out, they act as honey-guides, and for this purpose they have no doubt undergone special selection by the proper insects. The case is just analogous to that of the peacock's plumes or the wings of butterflies. In either instance, the spots and eye-marks tend to appear on the most highly-modified surfaces; but they are perpetuated and intensified by special selective action. Among birds and insects, sexual selection performs the work of fixing the colours; among flowers, the visits of bees and butterflies effect the same end. Lines are comparatively rare on regular flowers, but they tend to appear as soon as the flower becomes even slightly bilateral, and they point directly towards the nectaries. Hence they cannot be mere purposeless products of special modification; they clearly subserve a function in the economy of the plant, and that function is the direction of the insect towards the proper place for effecting the fertilization of the ovary. In the common rhododendron, the connection can be most readily observed with the naked eye, and the honey tested by the tongue. In this case, one lobe of the corolla secretes a very large drop of nectar in a fold near its base, and the lines of dark spots appear on this lobe alone, pointing directly towards the nectariferous surface.

The *Geraniaceæ* afford an excellent illustration of the general principle. They are on the whole a comparatively high family of polypetals, for their ovary tends to become compound and very complicated, and they have many advanced devices for the dispersion of their seeds. *Oxalis corniculata*, our simplest English form, is pale yellow: *O. acetosella* is white, with a yellow base, and its veins are delicately tinged with lilac. The flowers of *Erodium* and *Geranium*, which are much more advanced, are generally pink or purplish, often marked with paler or darker lines. For the most part, however, these regular forms are fairly uniform in hue; but many of the South African *Pelargoniums*, cultivated in gardens and hot-houses, are slightly bilateral, the two upper petals standing off from the three lower ones; and these two become at once marked with dark lines, which are in some cases scarcely visible, and in others fairly pronounced. From this simple beginning one can trace a gradual progress in heterogeneity of colouring, till at last the most developed bilateral forms have the two upper petals of quite a different hue from the three lower ones, besides being deeply marked with belts and spots of dappled colour. In the allied *Tropæolum* (Fig. 23) or Indian cress (the so-called nasturtium of old-fashioned gardens—though the plant is really no more related to the water-cress and other true nasturtiums than we ourselves are to the great kangaroo) this tendency is carried still further. Here, the calyx is prolonged into a deep spur, containing the honey, inaccessible to any but a few large insects; and towards this spur all the lines on the petals converge. Sir John Lubbock

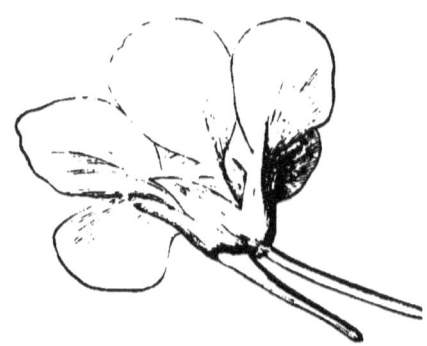

FIG. 23.—Flower of Indian cress (*Tropæolum majus*), with one sepal prolonged into a honey-bearing spur; orange and yellow.

observes that without such conventional marks to guide them, bees would waste a great deal of time in bungling about the mouths of flowers; for they are helpless, blundering things at an emergency, and never know their way twice to the same place if any change has been made in the disposition of the familiar surroundings.

The readiness with which the *Geraniaceæ* pass into irregular forms in *Pelargonium* and in the balsam genus (*Impatiens*), in itself shows that they are a fairly advanced family, and explains the common appearance of pink and purple petals among flowers which at a casual glance seem scarcely so much modified as the pinks or the crucifers.

The *Malvaceæ* are another family in which lines and stripes commonly occur; and they are shown to be of a comparatively advanced type by their peculiarly modified pistil, and by the union of their stamens into a tube, to which the petals adhere at the base. *Lavatera arborea* is purplish red; of our three

FIG. 24 —Flower of pink (*Dianthus*); pink, with lighter spots.

Malvæ, one, *M. rotundifolia*, is pale blue; *M. sylvestris* is purple; and *M. moschata*, rose-coloured, or, rarely, white. All have strongly-marked lines, and, in addition to this, the vivid green calyx, seen through the interstices of the petals, acts apparently as a supplementary honey-guide. The same peculiarities distinguish the genus *Althæa*, of which we have two species, *A. officinalis*, pale rose-colour, and *A. hirsuta*, purplish blue.

F

Among the very regular *Caryophyllaceæ*, the small, open *Alsineæ* are never spotted or variegated; and even in the more developed *Sileneæ*, with their tubular calyces, only the highest British genus, *Dianthus* (Fig. 24), ever has marks on its petals.

In most regular flowers, the lines are mere intensifications (or diminutions) of the general colouration along the veins or ribs of the corolla; and they point towards the base or claw of the petal, where the honey is usually secreted. But in irregular flowers, we often get a higher modification of colour, so that one region of the petal is yellow or white, while another is pink or blue; and these regions often run transversely, not longitudinally. Such modifications usually affect the most highly altered parts of the irregular flower.

The common wild pansy, *Viola tricolor*, affords a good example of complex variegation. Its flowers are purple, white, or yellow; or have these pigments variously intermixed. The two upper pairs of petals are usually the most coloured; the lower one is broadest, and generally yellow at the base, with dark lines leading toward the spur. *Viola palustris* exhibits the same tendency in a less degree; it is pale blue, with purple streaks. *V. canina* has hardly more than a few darker or lighter lines. The whole family is immensely interesting from the present point of view, and should be closely observed by the student at first hand. Its changes and varieties will be found full of instructive suggestions as to the origin and nature of colour modifications.

In *Polygala vulgaris*, the two coloured petaloid sepals, commonly called wings, are also delicately veined.

Among the *Papilionaceæ*, variegation and lines of colour are common in the higher genera, which are more strictly adapted to bees and other specialised honey-suckers, such as *Vicia, Lathyrus, Onobrychis*, &c. The standard is usually the most highly coloured; the wings and keel are generally paler, or one degree lower in the scale of progressive colouration. In *Lathyrus hirsutus, L. silvestris, Vicia Bithynica,* and *Astragalus alpinus*, this peculiarity is well marked. The cultivated sweet-pea, a Sicilian *Lathyrus*, illustrates the general principle even better than any of our native kinds.

Among regular *Corolliforæ*, variegation is not very common, though it occurs much oftener than in the polypetalous classes, especially at the throat of the tube, as in the forget-me-nots (*Myosotis*); but in irregular *Corolliflora* it is exceedingly frequent. The *Lentibulaceæ* and other small families afford several examples. In the great order of *Labiatæ*, the highly modified lower lip is very often spotted, especially where it is most developed. This is the case in *Stachys silvatica, Lamium purpureum, Galeopsis tetrahit, Calamintha acinos, Nepeta cataria, N. glechoma, Ajuga reptans, Scutellaria galericulata*, and many other species. Several exotic kinds show the same tendency in a more marked degree.

The *Scrophularineæ*, however, form perhaps the best example of any. It was noticed above that comparatively few of these are as blue or as purple as might be expected from their high organisation. The explanation is that they have mostly got beyond the monochromatic stage altogether, and reached the level of intense variegation. They are, in fact, a family with profoundly modified flowers (Fig. 25), most of which are very specially adapted to very exceptional modes of insect fertilisation. The *Veronicas* alone among our English genera are simply blue, with white or pink lines; the others are mostly spotted or dappled. *Antirrhinum majus* is purple, sometimes crimson or white, with the curiously closed throat a bright yellow. *Linaria cymbalaria* is blue or lilac, with white patches, and the palate a delicate primrose. *L. spuria* is yellow, with a purple throat. *L. minor* is purple, with a white lower lip and yellow palate.

FIG. 25.—Flower of toad flax (*Linaria vulgaris*), with corolla prolonged into a honey-bearing spur; yellow, with orange palate.

The very strange flowers of *Scrophularia* have a curious, indescribable mixture of brown, green, dingy purple, and buff. *Sibthorpia* is pink, with the two smaller lobes of the corolla yellow. *Digitalis purpurea*, the foxglove, is purple, spotted with red and white. *Euphrasia*, eye-bright, is white or lilac, with purple veins, and the middle lobe of the lower lip yellow. *Melampyrum arvense* is red, with pink lips and a purple throat. Description, indeed, is quite inadequate to convey any sufficient notion of the intimate intermixture of hues in most scrophularineous plants. As a rule, the spots or patches of intrusive colour are developed transversely near the palate or around the throat. Purple, red, or blue appear to be the prevalent ground-tones, with white and yellow introduced as contrasted tints to heighten the effect of the principal constructive parts.

Among Monocotyledons, such plants as the highly modified *Iris* genus show similar results. Our own *I. fœtidissima* has blue sepals, with yellow petals and

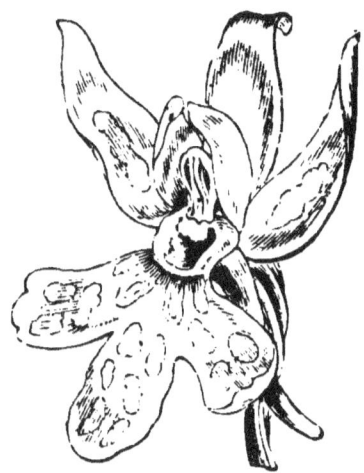

FIG 26.—Flower of spotted orchid (*Orchis maculata*); purple, dappled with pink and white.

spathulate stigmas, all much veined. The *Orchidaceæ* exhibit the same tendency far more markedly. *Orchis mascula, O. maculata, O. laxiflora,* and many other British species have the lip spotted (Fig. 26). In *O. militaris* and *O. hircina,* the variegation is even more conspicuous. In *O. ustulata,* the spots on the lip are raised. The problematical bee-orchid, *Ophrys apifera,* is singularly dappled on the lip and disk, and has the sepals different in colour from the rest of the flower. *Aceras anthropophora*, the man-orchid, has green sepals and petals, edged with red, and a yellow lip, pink fringed. *Cypripedium calceolus*, the lady's slipper, *Cephalanthera grandiflora*, white helleborine, and most other British species, are similarly very diversified in colour. As to the exotic species, some of them are more peculiarly tinted and blended with half a dozen different hues than any other forms of flowers in the whole world.

On the other hand, primitive yellow flowers of the earliest type never have any lines or spots whatsoever. We may therefore sum up the facts about variegation as follows:—

(1.) Very simple and primitive flowers are usually of one colour throughout.

(2.) Regular flowers of higher types are often marked by lines of a different colour or shade, which generally correspond with the venation of the petals.

(3.) Irregular flowers are often marked with distinct patches of different colour (sometimes transverse), which seem to act as honey-guides.

(4.) The most divergent colours usually appear on the most highly modified parts of the flower.

CHAPTER IV.

RELAPSE AND RETROGRESSION.

Flowers which have reached a given stage in the progressive scale of colouration often show a tendency to fall back to a lower stage. When this tendency is of the nature of a mere temporary reversion (that is to say, when it affects only a few individuals, or a casual variety), it may conveniently be described as Relapse. When, however, it affects a whole species, and becomes fixed in the species by a new and presumably lower adaptation, it may best be styled Retrogression. The difference between these two forms of reversion will become clearer after we have examined a few cases of each in detail.

Primary yellow flowers, like the buttercups, potentillas, and St. John's worts, show little or no tendency to vary in colour in a state of nature. They have never passed through any earlier stage to which they can revert; and they are not likely to strike out a new hue for themselves except through the action of some special differentiating circumstances, such as those ensured by cultivation.

Some white flowers, on the other hand, show a decided tendency occasionally to revert to yellow, especially in the simpler orders. *Erysimum orientale* varies from white to pale primrose. *Raphanus raphanistrum*, as already noted, is usually even lilac, often white, and on the sea-shore yellow. The white cistuses often revert to a pale sallow tinge. In some roses, the throat becomes yellow in certain specimens. Many umbellates vary from white to a faint yellowish green. In several other cases, stray yellow specimens of normally white species are not uncommon.

Pink and red flowers almost invariably revert in many individuals to white. Indeed, there is probably not a single blossom of these colours in England of which white specimens may not occasionally be gathered. A few typical instances must suffice. All the British roses are reddish pink or white. So are *Saponaria officinalis*, and many pinks. *Malva moschata* runs from rose-coloured to white; *M. rotundifolia* from pale lilac-pink to whitish. *Erodium cicutarium* has rosy or white petals; all the geraniums occasionally produce very pale flowers. White varieties of heaths are frequent in the wild state. Where the red or purple is very deeply engrained, however, as in labiates, reversion to white occurs less commonly. But almost all pink or red flowers become white with the greatest readiness under cultivation.

Blue flowers in nearly every case produce abundant red, pink, and white varieties in a state of nature. It would seem, indeed, as though this highest development of colour had not yet had time thoroughly to fix itself in the constitution of most species. In an immense number of cases, it still appears as a late modification of red, the bud or young petals being still of that colour, and only deepening into blue as the flower opens. Hence individual reversion is here almost universal as an occasional incident in every species. The columbine (*Aquilegia vulgaris*) is blue or dull purple, sometimes red or white. The larkspur (*Delphinium ajacis*) often declines from blue to pink or white. The monkshood (*Aconitum napellus*) is an extremely deep blue, very rarely white. White violets everybody knows well. The rampions (*Phyteuma*) vary from blue to white; so do many of the campanulas. *Gentiana campestris* is sometimes white. In most *Boragineæ*—for example, in borage, viper's bugloss, and forget-me-not—pink and white varieties are common. Pink and white *Veronicas* also occur in abundance among normally blue species. *Prunella vulgaris* occasionally produces rosy or white blossoms. White wild hyacinths are often gathered. Many other cases will suggest themselves to every practical botanist.

Blue flowers, however, very seldom revert to yellow, though this change takes place in some cultivated hyacinths, and somewhat differently in the pansy. As a rule, the blue goes back only as far as those shades from which it has more recently been developed. This is, perhaps, the true rationale of De Candolle's law of xanthic and cyanic types.

Sometimes, indeed, we may say that the new colour has not yet begun to fix itself in the species, but that the hue still varies under our very eyes. Of this the little milkwort (*Polygala vulgaris*) affords an excellent example, for it is occasionally white, usually pink, and frequently blue. Here we may fairly regard the pink as the normal hue, while the white is doubtless due to reversion, and the blue to progressive modification, not yet fully selected by insects; so that in all probability it is now actually in course of acquiring a new colour. Much the same thing happens with the common pimpernel (*Anagallis arvensis*). Its ancestral form is probably the woodland loosestrife (*Lysimachia nemorum*), for though the capsule of the pimpernel now opens transversely, it still retains the five dark lines which mark the primitive dehiscence; and in other respects it most closely resembles *Lysimachia*, which is a bright yellow. But pimpernel itself is usually orange-red, while a blue variety is frequent on the continent, and sometimes appears in England as well. Every botanist can add half a dozen equally good instances from his own memory.

Highly variegated flowers show the greatest tendency of any to such occasional reversions, or, as it is usually put, are extremely variable. The pansy (*Viola tricolor*) is an excellent example. The snapdragons, orchids, and irises are also cases in point.

Indeed, the extent to which flowers are modifiable in the hands of gardeners largely depends upon the amount of modification which they have already undergone in the natural condition. Very highly developed plants have on the one hand acquired a great constitutional plasticity of nature, and on the other hand have a large number of previous stages to fall back upon. Hence gardeners can do almost anything they like with *Dahlias*, *Cinerarias*, *Asters*, *Chrysanthemums*, and other advanced corymbiferous composites; with *Calceolarias*, *Antirrhinums*, and other *Scrophularineæ*; with pansies, pea-flowers, heaths, and lilies; with exotic *Gloxinias*, *Bignonias*, *Tecomas*, and *Gesnerias*. On the other hand, variegated or largely altered flowers of the simpler types rarely occur even in cultivation. Hence we may, perhaps, reasonably infer that great readiness to assume new colours affords in itself a certain slight presumption in favour of some previous colour modification. We shall apply this hypothetical principle in the sequel to sundry cases of yellow colouration in apparently high families, as one among several tests by which we may be aided in distinguishing retrograde from primitive yellowness.

This seems also the proper place to consider the proofs of the position already advanced, that new colours make their appearance at the edge of the petal, and gradually work their way inward. Four such proofs may be advanced. In the first place, purely adventitious individual colours almost always so appear. For example, the reddish tinge occasionally observed on many yellow flowers is usually at the tip: so is the lilac tinge on certain white anemones, and the pink tinge on many crucifers and umbellates. In the second place, the slight blush which occurs normally on flowers like the daisy, the apple-blossom, and the blackberry, and which appears to be as yet comparatively uninfluenced by insect selection, seeing that it is deepest on the back of the petals, generally occurs near the tip. The same peculiarity may be observed also in several small *Caryophyllaceæ*, *Papilionaceæ*, and *Ericaceæ*. In the third place, flowers which open pink, like so many *Boraginaceæ*, and then become blue, remain always red at the base, and only acquire the new hue in the expanded limb of the corolla. In tulips, *Hydrangea*, *Richardia*, &c., like facts occur.

And in the fourth place, white varieties of blue flowers usually have the centre bluish and the edge white; pink varieties have the centre bluish and the edge pink, and so forth. Here, we know what the normal colour is like, and can see that the new hue appears first at the periphery. For example, white violets, a variety of *Viola odorata*, have the spur and lower part of the petals blue or bluish; the whiteness only extends to the broad part of the petals. In a large number of varieties examined by the writer, the same law holds good. Hence we are justified to some extent in assuming that when a plant exhibits a different colour at the base and at the tip of the petal, the basal colour is probably more primitive than the peripheral one.

If we turn from the white violet, with its blue spur, to the very variegated pansy, we may perhaps ask ourselves which is the earlier of its colours, the purple, the white, or the yellow. But if we observe that the spur, unseen at the back of the flower, is usually deep violet blue, as are also the bases of the petals, while the yellow is usually found on the most expanded and modified part of the corolla, the lowest petal, and in its most nodal or functionally attractive part, just in front of the honey-cavity, we can hardly resist the inference thrust upon us by analogy—that the pansy was once all blue, and that the yellow has been developed here, as in the snapdragon and the ivy-linaria, to guide the bees to the proper place for securing the nectar and effecting cross fertilisation.

It is an interesting fact in this connection that an immense number of the very simplest flowers, when not themselves yellow, have yellow spots or patches at the bases of their petals. The reader is recommended to notice this point for himself in the commoner white or pink polypetalous flowers.

With the light thus cast upon the question to guide us, we may pass on to the general consideration of Retrogression in colours. Certain species of advanced families have apparently found it advantageous in certain circumstances regularly and consistently to revert to colours lower in the scale than the normal hue of their congeners. The reasons for such Retrogression are often easy enough to understand.

We may take the evening campion (*Lychnis vespertina*) as a good example (Fig. 15). This white flower, as we saw, is evidently descended from the red day campion (*Lychnis diurna*), because it is still often pale pink, especially towards the centre, verging into white at the edge. But it has found it convenient to attract moths and be fertilised by them ; and so it has lost its pinkness, because white is naturally the colour best seen by crepuscular insects in the dusky light of evening. It is scented at nightfall, and readily allures many moths by the combined attraction of sight and smell. Sir John Lubbock notes that such evening flowers never have any spots or lines as honey-guides on the petals, because such marks could not be seen at night, and would therefore be useless. All the other British species of *Lychnis* are red, pink, or purple.

The evening primrose (*Œnothera biennis*), now naturalised in England, is another excellent instance of the same sort. It belongs to the family of the *Onagraceæ*, which are highly evolved polypetalous plants, with the petals reduced to four or two in number, and placed above instead of below the ovary.

We should thus naturally expect them to be pink or lilac, and this is actually the case with most of our native species, the genus *Epilobium* having usually purple or red flowers, rarely white; while the smaller *Circæas* are pink or whitish. Why, then, is the evening primrose yellow? Because it is a night-flowering plant, fragrant in the evening, and its pale yellow colour makes it easily recognisable by moths. In this case, however, two points mark it off at once from the really primitive yellow flowers. In the first place, it has not the bright golden petals of the buttercup, but is rather more of a primrose tint; and this is a common distinguishing trait of the later acquired yellows. In the second place, it belongs to a genus in which red and purple flowers are common, whereas the buttercups are almost all yellow or whitey-yellow, and the potentillas mostly yellow or white. In short, primitive yellow flowers are usually golden, and belong to mainly yellow groups: reverted yellow flowers are often primrose, orange, or dull buff, and occur sporadically among blue, red, or purple groups.

There are other cases less immediately apparent than these. For instance, *Lamium galeobdolon*, a common English labiate, belonging to a usually purple or blue family, is bright yellow. But we can form some idea of how such changes take place if we look at the pansy, which we have seen reason to believe is normally violet-purple, but which usually has a yellow patch on the lowest petal. In the pansy's var. *lutea*, the yellow extends over the whole flower, no doubt because this incipient form has succeeded in attracting some special insect, or else grows in situations where yellow proves more conspicuous to bees than blue or purple. So, again, another English labiate, *Galeopsis tetrahit*, the hemp-nettle, has a pale purple or white corolla, sometimes with a tinge of yellow in the throat: and in the var. *versicolor*, the yellow spreads over all the flower, except a purple patch on the lower lip. In *G. ochroleuca*, the whole corolla has become pure yellow. In this way, one can understand the occurrence of such a flower as *Lamium galeobdolon*, especially since an allied species, *L. album*, is white, and all the genus is extremely variable in colour. Indeed, it is to be noted that the yellow labiates do not commonly occur among the less developed thymes, mints, and marjorams, but among the extremely specialised *Stachydeæ*, which have very modified flowers, and usually variegated or spotted lips. They seem to be essentially reversionary forms from purple or blue species, spotted with yellow. Nay, the lower lip of *L. galeobdolon* itself still shows marks of dark orange variegation, exactly answering to that of several purple *Lamiums*: and the base of the corolla tube is still pink or purplish.

Another hint of Retrogression is given us by flowers like our English balsams, *Impatiens noli-me-tangere* and *I. fulva*, in the fact that their yellow is generally dappled with numerous spots of deeper colour. The balsams are highly modified irregular *Geraniaceæ*, sepals and petals being both coloured: and at first sight it seems curious that our species should be yellow, while the simpler *Geraniums* and *Erodiums* are pink or red. But the genus as a whole contains many red and variegated species, and alters in colour with much plasticity under the hands of gardeners. *I. noli-me-tangere* is pale yellow spotted with red:

I. fulva is orange, dappled with deep brown. Both are almost certainly products of retrogressive selection.

Something of the same sort is seen in *Cheiranthus cheiri*, the wallflower. This large and highly developed stock-like crucifer is a peculiar yellowish brown in the wild state, frequently even primrose or primitive yellow. But it varies readily, often becoming red at the edges; and under cultivation it assumes numerous shades of red, purple, and brown. It appears to be a product of retrogressive selection from an original form like the European stock. This flower, combined with some others like *Adonis autumnalis, Ranunculus Ficaria*, and *Lotus corniculatus*, seems to suggest the idea that yellow may sometimes merge directly into red, without passing through the intermediate stages of white and pink. The other order would appear, however, to be the more regular and usual gradation.

In the *Primulaceæ*, we find similar instances. *Hottonia palustris*, a less developed form, is rosy lilac. *Cyclamen europæum* is white or rose-coloured. *Trientalis europæa* is white or pale pink, with a yellow ring. From such a stage as this, it is easy to get at our primroses, cowslips, and oxlips, which have pale yellow corollas, with orange spots at the throat. Indeed, one English species, *Primula farinosa*, is pale-lilac, with a yellow centre: and this might easily, under special circumstances, become pale primrose all over. The cultivated varieties of the cowslip, called Polyanthuses, readily assume various tints of orange, red, and pink, always at the edge, the deep yellow of the throat remaining unchanged. On the other hand, the yellow of the allied *Lysimachias* certainly appears to be primitive.

Among heaths, our only yellowish sort is the very degraded *Monotropa*, a leafless saprophyte of the lowest type, obviously a product of extreme Retrogression.

The colours of many *Scrophularineæ* may be explained in the same way. Perhaps the yellow of the mulleins is primitive; but as some species are white or purple, it is just as likely to be retrogressive. In *Linaria*, we may almost be sure that retrogression has taken place; for we can trace a regular gradation from lilac flowers with a yellow palate, like *L. cymbalaria*, to pale yellow flowers, like *L. vulgaris* (Fig. 25), which has the mass of the corolla primrose, and the palate orange. *Mimulus luteus* is also yellow, but it is usually marked inside with small purple spots, and sometimes has a large pink or red patch upon each lobe. In *Melampyrum cristatum*, the yellow corolla is variegated with purple: in *M. pratense*, it has the lip deeper in hue. All these genera include many purple and variegated species; and the yellow members almost always bear evident marks of being descended from polychromatic ancestors.

Among *Lentibulaceæ*, our debased *Utriculariæ* have pale yellow flowers; but *Pinguicula vulgaris* is bluish purple, and *Pinguicula lusitanica* yellow, tinged with lilac: so that here, too, we may suspect Retrogression.

The case of the yellow *Compositæ*, especially the *Ligulatæ*, is more difficult to decide. It would seem as though these plants, which have all their florets ligulate (Fig. 27), must be more highly developed than the *Corymbiferæ*, which have only the ray-florets ligulate, or than the *Cynaroideæ*, which have no ligulate florets at all. Hence we should naturally expect them to be blue or purple, whereas they are for the most part yellow of a very primitive golden type, while the ray-florets of the Corymbifers are usually white or pink, and all the florets of the Cynaroids are usually purple. It is, of course, quite possible that a flower might have progressed as far as the Corollifloral stage —might have joined all its petals into a united corolla under the influence of insect selection—and yet might

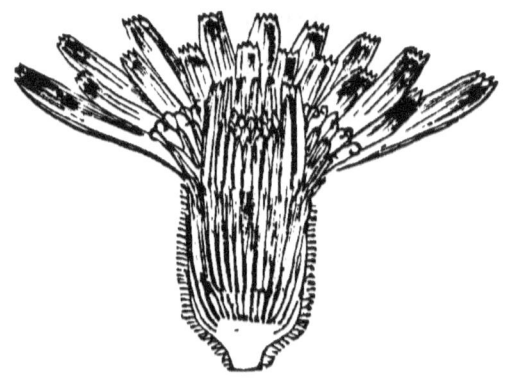

FIG. 27.—Vertical section of head of typical ligulate; yellow.

never have got beyond its primitive golden-yellow colouration. Something of the sort may be the case with *Chlora perfoliata* among the *Gentianaceæ*; it may even be the case with the *Lysimachia* genus among the *Primulaceæ*; and therefore it may also have been the case with the primordial ancestor of the *Compositæ*. But there are great difficulties in the way of this explanation. In the first place, it would be hard on that supposition to understand why the less-developed Cynaroids should have outstripped the more-developed Corymbifers and the most-developed

Ligulates. In the second place, it would be equally hard to understand why the most primitive Corymbifers, such as *Eupatorium*, should have purple or white florets, while the more developed genera, such as *Aster* and *Chrysanthemum*, should have most of them yellow. The following hypothetical explanation is suggested as a possible way out of this difficulty.

The primitive ancestral composite had reached the stage of blue or purple flowers while it was still at a level of development corresponding to that of the scabious or the *Jasione*. The universality of such colours among the closely allied *Dipsaceæ*, *Valeraineæ*, *Lobeliaceæ*, and *Campanulaceæ*, adds strength to this supposition. The central and most primitive group of composites, the Cynaroids, has kept up the original colouration to the present day; it includes most of the largest forms, such as the artichoke, and it depends most of any for fertilisation upon the higher insects. Very few of its members have very small florets. All our British species (except the degenerate *Carlina*) are purple, sometimes reverting to pale pink or white, while *Centaurea cyanus*, our most advanced representative of the tribe, rises even to bright blue.

Next to the Cynaroids in order of development come the Corymbifers, some of which have begun to develop outer ligulate rays. Here the least evolved type, *Eupatorium*, with few and relatively large florets, is usually purple or white, never yellow. But as the florets grew smaller, and began to bid for the favour of many miscellaneous small insects, reversion to yellow became general. In a few cases here and there we still find purple or white central florets, as in *Petasites vulgaris*, the butter-bur; but even then we get closely related forms, like *Tussilago farfara*, coltsfoot, which have declined to yellow. The smallest and most debased species, such as *Solidago virga-aurea*, golden rod, *Tanacetum vulgare*, tansy, and *Senecio vulgaris*, groundsel, have all their florets yellow and similar; unless, indeed, like *Gnaphalium* and *Filago*, cud-weed, *Artemisia absinthium*, wormwood, or *Xanthium strumarium*, burweed, they have declined as far as colourless or green florets, in which case they must be considered under our next head, that of Degeneration. On the other hand, the larger and better types of Corymbifers began a fresh progressive development of their own. In many *Senecios, Inulas, Chrysanthemums*, they produced yellow ray florets, similar in colour to those of the disk. In *Chrysanthemum leucanthemum, Anthemis cotula, Matricaria inodora*, &c., these rays, under the influence of a different type of insect selection, became white. In the daisy they begin to show signs of pink, and in the *Asters, Cinerarias*, &c., they have become lilac, purple, and blue. Complicated as these changes seem, they must yet have taken place two or three times separately in various groups of Corymbifers, for example in the *Asteroideæ*, the *Anthemideæ*, and the *Senecionidæ*.

The Ligulates were again developed from yellow-rayed Corymbifers by the conversion of all the disk florets into rays. Appealing for the most part to very large and varied classes of miscellaneous insects, they have usually kept their yellow colour; but in a few cases a fresh progressive development has been set up, producing the violet-blue or purple florets of the salsify (*Tragopogon porrifolius*), the deep blue *Sonchus alpinus*, and the bright mauve succory, *Cichorium intybus*. As a whole, however, the Ligulates are characterised by what seems a primitive golden yellow, only occasionally rising to orange-red or primrose in a few hawkweeds.

That this hypothetical explanation may be the true one seems more probable when we examine the somewhat similar case of the *Stellatæ*. Here it seems pretty clear that mere dwarfing of the flowers, by throwing them back upon earlier types of insect fertilisation, has a tendency to produce retrogression in colour. Even in the more closely allied *Dipsaceæ*, *Valerianeæ*, and *Campanulaceæ*, we see a step taken in the same direction, for while the large-flowered *Campanulas* and *Scabiosas* are bright blue, the smaller flowered teasel (*Dipsacus silvestris*) is pale lilac, the *Valerianas* are almost white, and the *Valerianellas* are often all but colourless. In the *Stellatæ*, the same tendency is carried even further. As a whole, these small creeping weeds of the temperate regions form a divergent group of the tropical *Rubiaceæ* (including *Cinchoniaceæ*), from which they are clearly derived as a degraded or dwarfed sub-order. Their square stems, their leaf-like interpetiolar stipules, and their usually lessened number of corolla-lobes, all point them out as derivative forms, not as survivals from an early ancestral type. Now, the tropical *Rubiaceæ* have tubular blossoms with long throats, and as a rule with five lobes to the corolla; but many of the Stellates have lost the tube and one corolla lobe. *Sherardia arvensis*, which has departed least of our British species from the norma of the race, has a distinct tube to the corolla, and is blue or pink. *Asperula*, which approaches nearer to the retrograde *Galiums*, has one pale lilac species and one white. The *Galiums* have no corolla-tube at all, and most of them are white; but two British species, *G. verum* and *G. cruciata*, are yellow, and one of these has become practically almost bi-sexual—a common mark of Retrogression. *Rubia peregrina* is even green. This clearly marked instance of Retrogression from blue through lilac and white to yellow makes the case of the Composites easier to understand. No doubt the dwarfed northern Stellates have found that they succeeded better by adapting themselves to the numerous small insects of the fields and hedgerows, and therefore have fallen back upon the neutral colours, white and yellow.

Something the same explanation may be hazarded in the case of the *Umbelliferæ*, a difficult family to deal with satisfactorily. It would be rash to assert that these curious flowers are descended from monopetalous ancestors, yet, with the analogy of *Galium* before our eyes, a suggestion to that effect may at least be entertained as possible. The relations of the *Umbelliferæ* with the *Araliaceæ* and *Corneæ* are very close; and it is difficult to believe that the last named family at least are not truly monopetalous. From the *Rubiaceæ*, indeed, a regular line of affinities leads us on through *Caprifoliaceæ* and *Corneæ* to *Umbelliferæ ;* and if we allow that *Galium* is descended from a tubular form like *Sherardia* it is hard to draw a line at such types as the elder, the wayfaring tree, the dogwood, or the ivy, till we arrive at the true umbellates themselves. Be this as it may, the family is one which clearly lays itself out to attract a large number of miscellaneous insects, as Müller has shown; and its prevailing colours are white and pale yellowish green. The flowers are all adapted to such small visitors as prefer these hues.

"The position of the honey on a flat disk," says Sir John Lubbock, "which renders it accessible to most insects, has the opposite result as regards the Lepidoptera, which therefore, as might naturally be expected, are but rare visitors of the *Umbelliferæ*. I have sometimes wondered whether the neutral tints of these flowers have any connection with the number of species by which they are frequented." This pregnant hint is full of meaning for the student of floral colouration.

After so many instances of more or less probable Retrogression, it will not surprise the reader to learn that in an immense number of other cases there is good reason to suspect some small amount of dwarfing or even Degeneration. These cases might perhaps be properly treated in the next chapter; but their connection with our present subject is so close that they fall into place more naturally here. It may have struck the reader, for example, when we were dealing with the Crucifers, that many of the smaller white forms were apparently lower in type than large and brilliant yellow flowers like the charlocks. That is quite true; but then, many of these small types are demonstrably dwarfed and slightly degraded, as, for example, *Cardamine hirsuta*, which has usually only four stamens instead of six, thus losing the most characteristic mark of its family. In *Senebiera didyma*, the petals have generally become quite obsolete; in some species of *Lepidium, Arabis, Draba,* &c., they are inconspicuous and often wanting. So in the smaller *Alsineæ* there are many signs of Degeneration. The normal forms of *Caryophyllaceæ* have two whorls of five stamens each; but these little creeping or weedy forms have often only one whorl, as in *Holosteum,* some *Cerastiums,* the smaller *Stellarias, Spergula, Polycarpon,* &c. In *Sagina, Cherleria,* and other very small types, the petals are often or always wanting. Indeed, most botanists will probably allow that nearly all our minute-flowered species, such as *Montia fontana, Claytonia perfoliata, Elatine hexandra, Radiola Millegrana, Circæa lutetiana, Ludwigia palustris, Peplis Portula, Tillæa muscosa, Myriophyllum spicatum, Hippuris vulgaris, Centunculus minimus,* and *Cicendia pusilla,* are distinctly degenerate forms. Though obviously descended from petaliferous ancestors, and closely allied with petaliferous genera or species, many of them have lost their petals altogether, while others have them extremely reduced in size. In several cases, too, the number of sepals, petals, or stamens has been lessened, and the plant as a whole has suffered structural degradations. Most of these dwarfed and degenerate flowers, if they have petals at all, have them white or very pale pink.

Readers of Sir John Lubbock's admirable little book on *British Wild-Flowers in Relation to Insects* will readily understand the reason for this change. They will remember that white flowers, as a rule, appeal to an exceptionally large circle of insect visitors, mostly of small and low grades. Hence, some among these very small flowers may often succeed, in certain positions, better than larger ones. Moreover, they will recollect that in numerous instances the larger blossoms of each family are so exclusively adapted to insect fertilisation that they cannot fertilise themselves; while among the smaller blossoms alternative devices for self-fertilisation commonly come into play after the flower has been open for some time, if it has not first been cross-fertilised. Structural considerations show us that in most such instances the larger and purely entomophilous flowers are the more primitive, while the smaller and occasionally self-fertilising flowers are derivative and degraded, having usually lost some of their parts. Hence, in tracing the progressive law of colouration in the families generally, it is necessary, for the most part, to consider only the larger and more typical species, setting aside most of the smaller as products of degeneration.

Moreover, as Mr. Henslow has shown, a large number of minute species have fallen back almost entirely upon self-fertilisation; and these, we must presume, when they retain their petals at all, retain them either by mere hereditary habit, as functionless relics, or else use them to effect an occasional cross at long intervals. Such degenerate and dwarfed species survive exactly as mites and other degraded forms survive in the animal world—because they fill certain holes and corners of the organic system better than more highly developed forms could do. The advantages of cross-fertilisation are seen in the large stature and vigorous constitution of the truly entomophilous or anemophilous plants, which have usurped all the best and richest places in nature, like dominant races that they are; the small degraded types are the species that have fallen behind in the struggle, and manage merely to eke out a precarious existence in the back slums of nature's economy.

CHAPTER V.

DEGENERATION.

The cases detailed in the last chapter lead us gradually up to the consideration of those very degenerate flowers whose structure has become completely debased, and especially of those which have green perianths instead of coloured corollas. As a rule, evolutionists have taken it for granted that green flowers were the earliest of any, and that from them the coloured types have been derived by insect selection. But if the principles laid down so far in this little treatise be correct, then it is obvious that, since all petals were originally yellow, green petals must be degraded, or at least altered types. Of course, the flowers of gymnosperms (in their blossoming stage) are mostly composed of green scales or leaves; and so it no doubt remains true that all flowers are ultimately descended from green, or greenish, ancestors. But if petals are by origin modified stamens, it will follow that all corollas at least were once coloured; and we shall probably see reason in the sequel to extend the principle to all perianths whatsoever. Without insisting upon the rule too dogmatically, so as to embrace every kind of angiosperm, we may, with some confidence, assert that wherever a flower possesses a rudiment of a perianth in any form, it is descended from coloured and entomophilous ancestors.

Those who have read Professor Ray Lankester's able little work on *Degeneration* will not be surprised to find that this retrograde agency has played as large a part in the vegetable as in the animal world. We will begin by examining some of the most certain cases, and then will proceed to those in which the evidence is more remote, and the traces of the original petaliferous structure more completely obliterated.

The Composites are, perhaps, in some respects, the very highest family of entomophilous flowers now existing on the earth. Their very structure implies the long and active co-operation of insect fertilisers. They could not otherwise have acquired the tubular form, the united corolla, the sheathed anthers, the compound heads of many-clustered florets. That originally green flowers could attain to this stage of development, and yet remain green, is simply inconceivable. But the Composites contain also some of the most degraded flower types in all nature. Beginning with such forms as the common groundsel (*Senecio vulgaris*), which has an inconspicuous yellow rayless head, specially adapted to self-fertilisation, we go on to plants like the *Artemisias*, with small greenish florets, which have taken, or are taking, to wind-fertilisation. Still more degraded are the *Gnaphaliums*, *Filagos*, and *Antennarias*, whose mode of fertilisation is problematical. And at the very bottom of the scale we get the little green *Xanthium;* so degenerate a form that its connection with the other

Composites can only be traced by means of several intermediate exotics, in every stage of progressive degradation. Such conclusive examples clearly show us that green flowers may occur as products of degradation even in the most advanced families.

Adoxa moschatellina is another excellent specimen of a green corollifloral blossom. This pretty little plant is closely allied to the honeysuckles and ivies; but it has somehow acquired a light green corolla, in place of a white or pink one. It is still entomophilous, and scantily secretes honey, so that the reason of the change cannot be immediately pointed out. Perhaps its very inconspicuousness saves it from the obtrusive visits of undesirable insect guests. The flowers of *Hedera helix*, common ivy, are also yellowish green. In the allied family of *Umbelliferæ* many flowers have declined to similar greenish tints; but this can hardly be their primitive colour, as they have an inferior ovary, which marks high development, even if they are not, as suggested, degenerate gamopetalous forms. *Smyrnium olusatrum* in this family, and *Chrysosplenium* among the *Saxifragaceæ*, exhibit very well the steps by which green corollas or perianths may be produced from originally white or yellow flowers. *Rubia peregrina* (wild madder) has also greenish monopetalous blossoms. All these are entomophilous. Their high structural development obviously negatives the notion that they are primitive green flowers; and we must necessarily conclude that they have become green for some special functional purpose of their own.

Among the highly developed *Ericaceæ*, greenish flowers occur in *Pyrola*, and to a less extent in

Arbutus and *Vaccinium*. *Pyrola*, at least, is a clearly degraded type.

The Orchids themselves, that most specialised of entomophilous types, show us other examples of flowers which have become more or less green; such as *Malaxis paludosa*, which has a yellowish tinge; *Liparis loeselii*, also yellowish; *Epipactis latifolia*, greenish brown; *Listera ovata*, grass-green; *Habenaria viridis*, yellowish green, and *Herminium monorchis*, pale greenish yellow. Why these highly-developed entomophilous blossoms should have found green suit them better than white, pink, or purple, it would be hard to say; but the fact remains indisputable; and it would be almost inconceivable that flowers of so high a type should have remained green all through the various stages of their long previous development. We may confidently set them down as products of incipient degeneration.

Among polypetalous flowers we get some equally interesting facts. Green appears as a variegation-colour on the highly-developed pea-flower, *Lathyrus silvestris*, and some others. *Helleborus viridis*, a doubtfully English ranunculaceous plant, has small green petals, employed as nectaries, and concealed by the large green sepals. It is entomophilous, and much visited by insects. Instead of being one of the least-developed *Ranunculaceæ*, however, it is one of the most advanced and highly differentiated types. In the lily family, again, the onion genus (*Allium*) is a small, and often degraded, group, whose more retrograde members produce green in place of purple or white flowers. In *Allium vineale*, and some others, the flowers often degenerate so far as to become small caducous bulbs. Here, degeneration is the only possible solution of the problem presented by the facts.

More frequently, however, reversion to wind-fertilisation (probably the primitive habit of all flowering plants) has produced green blossoms among angiosperms. This may result in two or three distinct ways. Either the corolla may become dwarfed and inconspicuous, or it may coalesce with the sepals or calyx-tube, or it may cease to be produced altogether. We may take the plaintains (*Plantago*) as a good example of the first-named case. Here we have tubular florets with four corolla-lobes, apparently descended from some form not unlike *Veronica* (though with four cells to the ovary) but immensely degraded. The corolla is thin and scarious, and its lobes are tucked away at the sides, so as not to interfere with the stamens and style. These, again, as in most wind-fertilised plants, hang out freely to the breeze; so that the whole spike when flowering shows no signs of a corolla from without, but seems to consist entirely of scales, stamens, and styles, just like a sedge or grass-plant. The expensive display of petals is no longer useful to the plant, which, therefore, economises the material that would otherwise be employed to allure the insects. It is impossible, however, to examine the functionless corolla without coming to the conclusion that *Plantago* must be descended from an entomophilous ancestor. Indeed, *P. media* still to some extent lays itself out to attract small flies, by which it is even now often visited and fertilised.

More degraded still is the allied *Littorella*, which

leads on to the very degenerate types of water-plants.

The *Rosaceæ* offer some good examples of green flowers in which the petals have become quite extinct. Some of them are entomophilous, and some anemophilous. *Alchemilla vulgaris* (lady's mantle, Fig. 28) is one of the former class. It is a degraded representative of the same group as agrimony; but it has lost its petals altogether. That it is a late, not a primitive

FIG. 28.—Flower of lady's mantle (*Alchemilla*), with double calyx, but no petals; green.

form, is shown by its very reduced carpels, and its small number of stamens. *Alchemilla arvensis* (parsley-piert) is an extremely debased moss-like descendant of some similar ancestor. It has tiny green petalless axillary flowers, self-fertilised, but occasionally visited by minute insects. Not far from these may be placed *Poterium sanguisorba* (Fig. 29), another degraded type, which has become anemophilous. This flower, too, is green, and has no petals; it usually possesses but one carpel, and it is altogether a clearly debased bisexual form. Its stamens are numerous, and they hang out to the wind, as do also the feathery stigmas in the female flowers, to catch the pollen from neighbouring heads. But the closely-allied *Sanguisorba officinalis* (Fig. 30) is evidently an entomophilous variation on the same ancestral form; for it resembles *Poterium* in every respect except in its flowers, which have very few stamens, enclosed in the purple calyx-tube. This interesting case shows us that when a flower has once lost its

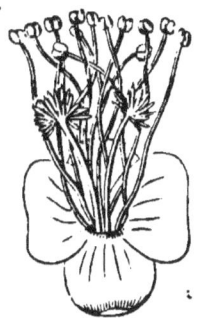
Fig. 29.—Flower of salad burnet (*Poterium sanguisorba*); green and anemophilous.

Fig. 30.—Flower of great burnet (*Sanguisorba officinalis*); purple and entomophilous.

petals and become anemophilous, it cannot re-develop them if it reverts to insect fertilisation, but must acquire a coloured calyx instead. The same lesson is perhaps elsewhere enforced by *Glaux maritima* among the *Primulaceæ*, and by *Clematis* among the *Ranunculaceæ*.

Mr. Darwin remarks that anemophilous flowers never possess a gaily-coloured corolla. The reason is clear. Such an adjunct could only result in the attraction of stray insects, which would uselessly eat up the pollen, and so do harm to the plant. Hence

H

when flowers revert to wind-fertilisation, both disuse and natural selection cause them to lose their petals, and become simply green.

In practice, however, it is often hard to distinguish between the casually entomophilous, the self-fertilised, and the really anemophilous species; and they are so intermixed that it may perhaps be best to consider them together. For example, the common ash (*Fraxinus excelsior*, Fig. 31) belongs to a gamopetalous family, the *Oleaceæ*, and is closely related to the white privet (*Ligustrum vulgare*), which has conspicuous

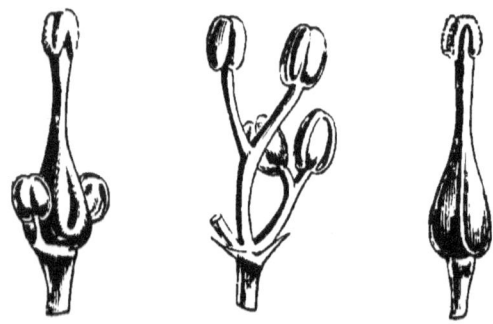

FIG. 31.—Hermaphrodite, male and female flowers of English ash (*Fraxinus excelsior*); purplish—no petals.

white flowers. But many large trees, owing, perhaps, to their long life, and consequent less necessity for producing many seeds, tend to lose their petals; and this is remarkably the case among the olive group. The shrubby species have usually flowers with a four-lobed corolla; and so have many of the southern arboreal forms (Fig. 32): but the northern trees, like our ash, have lost both calyx and corolla altogether, each naked flower consisting only of two stamens, with a single ovary between them. In appearance their blossoms seem of much the same sort as the wind-fertilised catkins and oak-kinds. Nevertheless, they are entomophilous, for their pollen, their arrangement in large masses, and their dark purple colour, sufficiently serve to entice numerous insects.

The spurges (*Euphorbiaceæ*) are a very interesting family of the same sort, exhibiting every gradation from perfect corolliferous blossoms to the most degraded flowers in all nature. Our English species have no true petals; but some exotic forms are truly

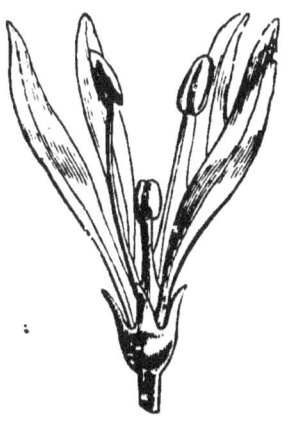

FIG. 32.—Hermaphrodite perfect flower of South European flowering ash (*Fraxinus ornus*); white, with four-lobed corolla.

dichlamydeous; and from them we can trace a gradual decline, through plants like dog's mercury (Figs. 33 and 34, *Mercurialis perennis*), which has a green calyx, but no corolla, to very degenerate green blossoms like our own spurges (*Euphorbia*), which consist of several extremely simplified flowers, collected together in a common involucre (Fig. 35). Each separate male floret is here reduced to a single stamen, raised on a short peduncle, and with a distinct joint at the spot where the petals once stood. It is worthy of notice, too, that when these degenerate, but still entomophilous, green flowers have found it desirable to attract insects

Fig. 33.—Male flower of dog's mercury (*Mercurialis*); green.

Fig. 34.—Female flower of dog' mercury (*Mercurialis*); green.

by developing new coloured surfaces in place of the lost corolla, they have not done so by producing a fresh set of petals, but have acquired coloured bract

Fig. 35.—Inflorescence of spurge (*Euphorbia*), the male flowers reduced to a sing stalked stamen, the female flowers to a naked ovary; green.

or involucres instead, as in the well-known *Iatropha* and *Poinsettias* of our hot-houses. This instance i exactly analogous to that of the *Sanguisorba*, considered above. It tends to show that petals are not developed from bracts, but from altered stamens.

From cases like these, we go down insensibly through all the ranks of the dicotyledonous *Monochlamydæ*. In the *Paronychiaceæ*, for example, we get an order closely allied to the *Caryophyllaceæ* (especially to *Polycarpon*); and in one genus (*Corrigiola*) the flowers have small white petals, which certainly aid in attracting insects. But in *Herniaria* the flowers are quite green, and the petals are reduced to five small filaments, thus partially reverting to their presumed original character as stamens. In *Scleranthus* the filaments are often wanting, and in some exotic species altogether so. The *Amarantaceæ*, unrepresented in Britain, approach the last-named family very nearly, but have the petals altogether obsolete; and in many cases, such as Prince's feather (*Amaranthus hypochondriacus*) and Love-lies-bleeding (*A. caudatus*), the calyx becomes scarious and brightly coloured. The *Chenopodiaceæ* are other near relations, in which also the petals are quite obsolete; and in most of them the perianth (or calyx) is green. In *Salicornia* it has become so embedded in the succulent leafless stem as to be almost indistinguishable. The *Polygonaceæ*, on the other hand, are a group of plants, allied to *Chenopodiaceæ*, but with a row of degraded petals, and a strong tendency to produce coloured perianths, analogous to that which we observed in *Sanguisorba*. The flowers of *Rumex*, the docks, are sometimes green, sometimes red; those of *Polygonum* are pale-green, white, or pink. *Rumex* is sometimes, *Polygonum* constantly, fertilised by insects.

Submerged or floating plants especially tend as a rule to become green-flowered, and to grow very degraded in structure. As instances, we may take *Myriophyllum*, *Ceratophyllum*, *Elodea*, *Lemna*, *Callitriche*, *Potamogeton*, *Ruppia*, and *Hippuris*. In most of these groups the proofs of great degeneration are too obvious to need insisting upon.

There remain doubtful, then, among green Dicotyledons, only the highly anemophilous families, like the nettles (*Urticaceæ*), and the catkin-bearing trees (*Amentiferæ*). The former have a well-developed calyx, at least to the male flowers; and it is difficult to see how any one who compares them with *Scleranthus* or *Mercurialis*, known descendants of petaliferous forms, can doubt that they too are degenerate types. Indeed, the mere fact that the stamens are opposite to the lobes of the calyx (Fig. 36), instead of alternate with them, in itself shows that a petal-whorl has been suppressed; as is likewise the case in the goose-foots and many other doubtful instances. Moreover, the nettles are closely allied to the elms (*Ulmaceæ*), which are obviously degenerate, and have acquired a coloured perianth, side by side with their resumption of the entomophilous habit.

As to the *Amentiferæ*, *Cupuliferæ*, and other catkin-bearers, at first sight we might suppose them to be primitive green anemophilous orders. But on closer consideration, we may see grounds for believing that they are really degenerate descendants of entomophilous plants. In the alder (*Alnus*) the male catkins consist of clustered flowers, three together under a bract, each containing a four-lobed perianth, with four stamens within (Fig. 37). These little florets exactly resemble, on a smaller scale, those of the nettle; and the stamens here, again, are opposite to the calyx-lobes, which of course implies the suppression

FIG. 36.—Male flower of nettle (*Urtica dioica*); green, with stamens opposite the sepals.

of a corolla. In the beech (*Betula*) the three florets under each bract are loosely and irregularly arranged; and in the male hornbeam (*Carpinus*) and hazel (*Corylus*) the perianth is wholly obsolete. All these are

FIG. 37.—Flowers of alder (*Alnus*); green, with stamens opposite the sepals.

probably quite anemophilous. The willows (*Salix*), on the other hand, though included by Sir John Lubbock in the same category (doubtless through inadvertence) have really become once more entomophilous; and they are much visited by bees, which obtain honey from the small glands between the florets and the axis (Figs. 38 and 39). Degenerate as these last-named species undoubtedly are, they may be connected by a regular line of illustrative examples (not genetically) through the beech, alder,

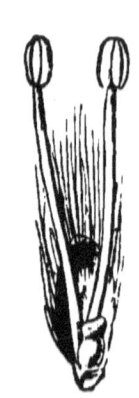
Fig. 38.—Male flower of willow (*Salix*); greenish.

Fig. 39 —Female flower of willow (*Salix*); greenish.

nettle, goosefoot, *Scleranthus*, *Herniaria*, and *Corrigiola*, with such perfect petaliferous types as the pinks, and ultimately the buttercups.

Among Monocotyledons, the very degraded little entomophilous flowers of the *Arum* (Fig. 40), enclosed in their green spathe, are often spoken of as though they represented a primitive type. In reality, however, they are degenerate dichlamydeous blossoms, linked to the lilies by *Acorus* (Fig. 41), which has numerous hermaphrodite flowers, each with a perianth of six scales, two rows of stamens, and a two-celled or three-celled ovary. Here, again, the green flower is obviously of late date.

What, then, are we to say about the anemophilous Monocotyledons, the great families of the sedges and grasses? Surely these, at least, are primitive green wind-fertilised flowers. Dogmatically to assert the contrary would, indeed, be rash with our existing

FIG. 40.—Spike or spadix of cuckoo-pint (*Arum maculatum*), consisting of numerous naked male, female, and neuter flowers, in separate clusters; purplish green.

FIG. 41.—Single floret of sweet sedge (*Acorus*), with six perianth pieces, six stamens, and an ovary; greenish yellow.

knowledge; yet we may see some reason for believing that even these highly anemophilous types are degenerate descendants of showy petaliferous blossoms. For, if the origin here assigned to petals be correct, it becomes clear that the *Juncaceæ*, or rushes, are only *Liliaceæ* in which the perianth has become dry and scarious; for the absolute homology of parts in the two orders cannot, of course, be denied. Some rushes, such as *Luzula*, approach very closely in general character to the grasses; and they also show themselves to be higher types by the further development of the ovary, and the decreased number of seeds. *Eriocaulon* and the *Restiaceæ* give us a further step towards the grass-like or sedge-like character. Some of the *Cyperaceæ* show apparent relics of a perianth in the bristles which surround the ovary, especially in *Scirpus* (Fig. 42);

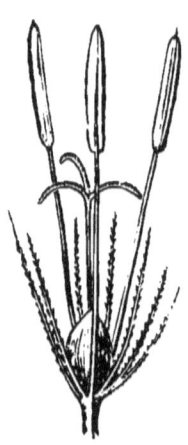

FIG. 42.—Flower of a sedge (*Scirpus*), with six hypogynous bristles, representing the calyx and corolla.

and perhaps the perigynium of *Carex* may represent a tubular perianth, though this is far more doubtful. In the grasses (*Gramineæ*) the perianth is either altogether obsolete, or else is reduced to the paleæ with the hypogynous scales or lodicules (Fig. 43). According to the most probable view (Fig. 44), the two paleæ represent the calyx (for the inner palea exhibits rudiments of two sepals, thus making up, with the outer palea, a single trinary whorl); while the lodicules represent two of the petals, the third (the inner one) being usually obsolete. It is fully developed, however, in the bamboo. The connection is here less clearly traceable than in the *Amentiferæ*, but it is still quite distinct enough to suggest at least the possibility that even grasses and sedges are ultimately derived from entomophilous flowers.

There is, however, another and more powerful argument against the idea that any of these existing green

FIG. 43.—Flower of grass, showing two lodicules or rudimentary petals three stamens, and ovary with two styles. One petal and one style are abortive.

flowers are really primitive. For what are the known marks of the most primitive existing flowers? Numerous simple superior carpels; distinct flowers on separate peduncles; no specialised bracts, no heads, no complications of any sort. And what are the known marks of late and more developed or degraded flowers? Unification of the pistil by union or suppression of the carpels; grouping of flowers in heads; separation of sexes; multiplication of accessory parts,

involucres, bracts, glumes, glands, awns, and so forth.
Now, to which of these classes do the yellow flowers
ordinarily belong? Clearly to the first. To which
do the green flowers ordinarily belong? Clearly to
the second. The organisation of the catkins, the
sedges, and the grasses is exactly analogous to that
of the spurges, which we know by an unbroken line
of intermediate links to be descended from petaliferous ancestors. The inference is almost irresistible

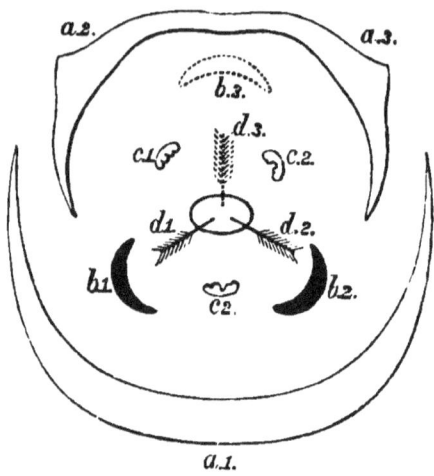

FIG. 44.—Diagram of flower of grass. a, sepals; a 1, outer sepal, flowering glume, or outer palea; a 2 and a 3, inner sepals, combined into a single inner palea; b, petals; b 1 and b 2, the lodicules; b 3, suppressed; c, stamens, all present; d, styles or stigmas; d 1 and d 2, present; d 3, suppressed. The whole inner side of the flower is thus abortive.

that so highly complicated a flower as that of the
grasses, with its one-celled, one-ovuled ovary, its two
styles, and its advanced paraphernalia of lodicules,
paleæ, and glumes, arranged in long and subdivided
spikes, must be a very specialised or degenerate, not
a primitive or early type. The more closely we
examine green flowers, the more do we see that
they form the opposite pole to such simple and truly

primitive forms as the buttercups, the potentillas, the *Alismaceæ*, and the simpler lilies of the *Gagea* type.

Thus we are led, at last, to the somewhat unexpected conclusion that anemophilous angiosperms are later in development than entomophilous angiosperms, and are derived from them. Though the earliest flowering plants—the pines, cycads, and other gymnosperms—were undoubtedly anemophilous from the first, yet the probability seems to be that all angiosperms were originally entomophilous, and that certain degenerate types have taken later on either to self-fertilisation, or to fertilisation by means of the wind. Why this apparently retrograde change has proved beneficial to them it would be impossible properly to inquire at the close of a work devoted to the simple question of the colours of flowers. We must content ourselves with noting that such degraded green flowers fall for the most part under one or other of four heads : (1) dwarfed or weedy forms; (2) submerged or aquatic forms ; (3) forest trees ; (4) grass-like or plaintain-like plants of the open wind-swept plains. That there are *no* primitive families of green or anemophilous angiosperms, it might perhaps be rash and premature to assert ; but at least we may assume as very probable the principle that wherever green flowers possess any perianth, or the relic or rudiment of any perianth, or are genetically connected with perianth-bearing allies, they have once possessed coloured insect-attracting corollas. In short, green flowers seem always (except in gymnosperms) to be the degenerate descendants of blue, yellow, white, or red ones.

CHAPTER VI.

MISCELLANEOUS.

A FEW general hints upon various side questions may here be conveniently thrown together in concluding our hasty survey. They must be accepted in most cases merely as suggestions for observation on the reader's own part. The subject is still a new one, and only vague ideas can as yet in certain directions be formulated upon it.

We have seen in several cases already that flowers which have lost their corolla often tend to re-develop brilliant colours in their calyx, as in *Sanguisorba;* while flowers which have lost both corolla and calyx often tend to re-develop such colours in bracts, involucres, or leaves, as in *Iatropha* and *Poinsettia*. Among our British *Monochlamydæ* there are comparatively few instances of such coloured calyxes, *Glaux*, *Daphne mezereum*, and *Ulmus*, being our best examples; but in many well-known exotic species, such as *Mirabilis dichotoma*, marvel of Peru, and the *Begonias*, the calyx is quite as beautifully coloured as any corolla. In *Bougainvillea*, three lilac bracts form the attractive organ. In *Aristolochia*, the tubular calyx simulates an irregular corolla, and in *A. cordata* it is large and brilliantly scarlet. In *Richardia africana*, the so-called Æthiopian lily, the spathe, surrounding a spike of very degraded achlamydeous flowers, is pure white, and very attractive. *Amherstia nobilis*, *Bromelia pinguin*, several species of *Salvia*, and many other exotics, have handsome bracts, which add greatly to their beauty.

The fact that in such cases flowers do not develop new petals from bracts or leaves, but acquire instead coloured calyxes or involucres, goes to prove the validity of the view with which we set out, that petals are really altered stamens, not altered leaves or sepals. For if they could once be developed from leaves, there would be no reason why they should not be developed from them here again. But if they were developed from stamens, and then lost in these instances, we could easily understand why the plant could not afford to waste any more of its now diminished number of stamens for purely attractive purposes, and so was forced to pour the necessary pigment for alluring insects into the other surrounding organs. In other words, on the Wolfian principle, there would be no reason why flowers with petals should not appear sporadically among monochlamydeous families; on the principle here advocated, it is quite clear why stray entomophilous species, developed from these degraded types, should have coloured calyxes, instead of coloured petals.

Among highly-developed, or succulent plants, the calyx and bracts often tend to assume colours like those of the petals, as do also the peduncles and the stem. Cases occur in *Ajuga reptans*, *Echium*, *Sedum*, and *Rumex*, among British plants; and more noticeably in *Peperomia, Echeveria, Epiphyllum*, and other exotics. The calyx and the expanded stipules which cover the young flower-heads in red clover (*Trifolium pratense*) and many other clovers, are delicately pink or purple. In *T. arvense* the sepals are pale lilac, and in *T. incarnatum* pale yellow. The whole upper portion of the flowering stem in *Chrysosplenium* is bright golden.

Where the calyx is largely exposed to view, as in the globe-flower (*Trollius*), the columbine, the hellebores, and the monkshood, it is apt to become quite as brilliant as the petals. In such cases its colouration usually follows the same law of progressive development as the corolla. Sometimes, under these circumstances, the now almost useless petals are suppressed altogether, as in *Caltha*, a near relative of *Trollius*, as well as in the *Anemones* and *Clematis*. At other times they are utilised as nectaries, as in columbine, hellebore, and monkshood. In the meadow-rues (*Thalictrum*) the petals are suppressed, and the sepals very small, so that the flower depends for attractiveness almost entirely upon its clustered yellow stamens. In *Impatiens, Polygala*, and some other British genera, sepals and petals share almost equally in the attractive display.

Where the petals have become much dwarfed, the calyx is apt to aid them, if brilliant colouration again becomes necessary. For example, our own wild gooseberry, wild currant, and most other members of the *Ribes* genus, have very inconspicuous petals; but in the North American scarlet Ribes of our gardens (*R. sanguineus*), the flower has re-assumed a brilliant colouring, and it has done so by making its calyx bright red, instead of by increasing the size and deepening the hue of its small white petals. In the *Fuchsia*, the *Hydrangea*, and many other well-known exotics, we get exactly similar devices.

Parasites and saprophytes do not as a rule require to produce green leaves; hence, most of them, like *Cuscuta, Orobanche, Lathræa*, and *Monotropa*, have the stem and leaves (or scales) coloured like the flowers. Imperfect parasites which contain chlorophyll, however, have the leaves more or less green, as in *Viscum, Bartsia, Rhinanthus*, and *Melampyrum*.

The outer florets of compound heads are apt to produce larger petals than the inner ones, as in many Umbellates (like cow-parsnip), the guelder-rose, the *Hydrangea*, and the rayed forms of Composites. These are obviously intended to increase the total attractive effect. In the Umbellates and in candytuft the outer petals of the individual flowers grow longer than the inner ones.

Petals have perhaps been independently developed from stamens at least twice over, once in the Dicotyledons, and once in the Monocotyledons. Insects, having once learnt to visit coloured surfaces in search of pollen and honey, would naturally tend to visit all such surfaces in future, and thus to select for fertilisation any coloured flowers that offered them any attraction in the way of food, of whatsoever sort. Apparently, at last one species of gymnosperm, the larch (*Pinus larix*), has thus become entomophilous, its fertile scales being interspersed with bright pink or red empty bracts, which seem to subserve an attractive function. They are certainly visited by insects, perhaps in search of some secretion from the bracts. This case may be looked upon as analogous to those of the ripe cones in the juniper and yew, which have similarly assumed the guise of attractive fruits, eaten by birds, who disperse their seeds. Such gymnosperms may be said metaphorically to have taken a hint from the angiosperms about them, and have acted upon it for their own advantage.

It has been assumed throughout that the progressive modification of the colours of petals is due in the main to increased oxidation of their contents. It may be added here that the thin edges of the petals where the newer colours usually first make their appearance, are the parts where oxidation would most naturally take place. Hence, probably, the distinct analogy between fading colours and progressive colours. In most cases, colours appear most vividly on the outside of the petals, where they were exposed in the bud, and where oxidation would most readily occur. The red tinge on the outside of daisies, apple-blossom, &c., is here once more very significant. In *Convolvulus arvensis* the mass of the corolla is white; but the lines exposed in the bud are deep pink, evidently from oxidation; and at the same time they form excellent honey-guides of the ordinary simpler sort. In many others of the same genus a similar result may be observed. The under side of the petals in St. John's worts, and the back of the standard in *Lotus*, are frequently ruddy red. The outer glumes of grasses are often purplish; the fruiting perianths of *Rumex* grow red as they ripen. Put beside the rosy cheeks of peaches, apples, and many other fruits, and the obvious oxidation colours of injured parts and autumn leaves, these facts are full of functional significance.

In a single flower, the common pink *Phlox*, a change apparently takes place in the reverse order to that laid down in this treatise as the general law, for it presents early in the morning a light blue tint, and retrogrades to pink as the sun advances in the sky. But it has been suggested (quite apart from our present theory) that the blue colour is due to the presence of some substance which becomes blue by non-elimination of oxygen during the night; and as the oxygen is given out during the day, the blue colour disappears. If this theory be well founded, the apparent exception really confirms our rule.

It has been objected by two or three authoritative critics that the original petals need not necessarily have been yellow, because they represent the flattened filament, not the anthers; and it is the pollen that gives the yellow colour to most stamens. But it may be answered that in the primitive yellow flowers (for example, the buttercups) the filaments are usually of the same golden yellow as the petals; and in many other flowers they retain more or less of a yellowish tinge. In white flowers they show a strong tendency to become white; but in pink and blue ones, pink or blue filaments are comparatively rare. Sometimes, indeed, the filaments become brightly coloured, so as to share in the attractive display; as a rule, however, they are yellow in the yellow flowers, white or greenish-yellow, with more or less of a pinky tinge, in almost all others. The subject is certainly one which requires further investigation.

According to Sachs, the yellow pigment of the

flowers here described as primitive is usually identical in composition with the ordinary yellow chlorophyll of leaves, while the orange, pink, red, and blue pigments are of more elaborate kinds.

If the botanical reader will provisionally accept the principles laid down in this little book, and will then test their validity by applying them to the flowers which he meets in his daily walks, he will find that many other confirmatory examples occur to him at every step, most of which are too numerous to insert here. He will also often find that close inspection reveals some unexpected answer to a superficial difficulty, some solution for the problem of an apparent exception, which can only be obtained by personal examination of the specimen with that particular object held definitely in view. For example, the case of the dead-nettle (*Lamium album*) was cited above as one of a labiate grown white by reversion (Fig. 45). This may have seemed at the time a purely gratuitous and arbitrary supposition. Why should not the white form be primitive, and the purple or pink ones be derived from it? But if the flower of a dead-nettle be carefully examined, it will be found in most cases to be not purely white, but to have some dusky lines and markings on its lower lip, of a pale brown or dim grey-black, which exactly answer to those on the lip of *L. maculatum*, and in a less degree of *L. purpureum*. Now, such markings do not occur among original white flowers like the crucifers and *Caryophyllaceæ*; but they are common on the lower lip of purple labiates. Moreover, we know that *Lamium maculatum* is very closely allied to *L. album*, and that it is purple-red instead of white. Both have the leaves occasionally marked in the centre with a white line or spot, which is a symptom of very close relationship. Indeed, Mr. Bentham formerly united the two in a single species; and even now he is doubtful whether they should be regarded as more than mere varieties. When we consider that all purple labiates are liable to be spotted with white; that the purple and white forms are here closely allied; that in *Galeopsis tetrahit* we

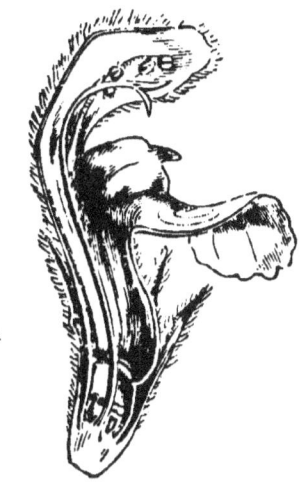

FIG. 45.--Vertical section of dead-nettle (*Lamium album*); white, with dark lines.

have a regular gradation from pure purple flowers to almost pure yellow ones; that in *Lamium galeobdolon* we have a related yellow form similarly spotted; that all the *Lamiums* show a tendency to variegation; and that the white flower has itself an inconspicuous and probably functionless variegation, where the purple one has conspicuous and useful honey-guides, the inference is almost irresistible that the common white form, *L. album*, represents a retrogressive modification of the rarer and obsolescent purple form, *L. maculatum*.

It would, of course, be impossible to treat every similar instance at equal length without swelling this volume to an unreasonable extent. But if the reader will carefully examine, at first hand, all cases of what seem to him adverse examples, he will usually find some such hint of the true relation, surviving in the flower itself. Excellent studies may thus be made of *Teucrium scorodonia*, compared with our three other British *Teucriums* (where the calyx suggests the relative stages of development); of *Ajuga chamæpitys* with *A. reptans*; of our three *Melampyrums*; of *Rhinanthus* and *Pedicularis*, and of the various *Linarias*. The *Orobanches* are also full of instructiveness, as are likewise *Pinguicula* and *Utricularia*. The descriptions given in Floras and other botanical works, and even the best coloured plates, supply very inadequate ideas of the minute observation involved in the study of this subject from the evolutionary point of view. Dried specimens are of course almost useless. The investigation must be conducted upon the living corolla in all stages of its development. Those who will take the trouble thus to watch the actual growing flowers for themselves will soon learn to recognise many other little marks of relative progress or retrogression which cannot all be set down definitely in black and white without unnecessary and tedious prolixity.

If the general principle here put forward is true, the special colours of different flowers are due to no mere spontaneous accident, nay, even to no meaningless caprice of the fertilising insects. They are due in their inception to a regular law of progressive modification ; and they have been fixed and stereotyped in each species by the selective action of the proper beetles, bees, moths, or butterflies. Not only can we say why such a colour, once happening to appear, has been favoured in the struggle for existence, but also why that colour should ever make its appearance in the first place, which is a condition precedent to its being favoured or selected at all. For example, blue pigments are often found in the most highly-developed flowers, because blue pigments are apparently a natural product of high modification —a simple chemical outcome of certain extremely complex biological changes. On the other hand, bees show a marked taste for blue, because blue is the colour of the most advanced flowers ; and by always selecting such, where possible, they both keep up and sharpen their own taste, and at the same time give additional opportunities to the blue flowers, which thus ensure proper fertilisation. May we not say that it ought always to be the object of naturalists in this manner to show not only why such and such a " spontaneous " variation should have been favoured whenever it occurred, but also to show why and how it could ever have occurred at all ?

THE END.

London:
R. CLAY, SONS, AND TAYLOR,
BREAD STREET HILL, E.C.

www.ingramcontent.com/pod-product-compliance
Lightning Source LLC
Chambersburg PA
CBHW021941160426
43195CB00011B/1174